Days of Transformation
By remote coaching

Guðbjörn Gunnarsson

Days of Transformation: By Remote Coaching

Publisher: Guðbjörn Gunnarsson

Copyright © 2025 by Guðbjörn Gunnarsson

Contact Information: hvatning1@gmail.com

All rights reserved.

No part of this book may be reproduced in any form or by any electronic or mechanical means, including information storage and retrieval systems, without written permission from the author, except for the use of brief quotations in a book review.

ISBN 979-8308-8-5700-6

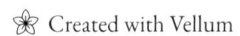

❦ Created with Vellum

Contents

Introduction — 5

1. Day 1 — 15
   Execution is the Motivation
2. Day 2 — 23
   The Mastery League – Living Life Like a Champion
3. Day 3 — 33
   Time – Slowing Down, Savoring, and Harnessing Life's Most Precious Resource
4. Day 4 — 41
   Designing Your Health Box
5. Day 5 — 51
   The Mind – Enhancing Awareness and Mastering Your Thoughts
6. Day 6 — 61
   Knowledge for the Mind, Experience for the Body – Building a New Personality
7. Day 7 — 69
   The 5% Syndrome – Upgrading the Mind's Operating System
8. Day 8 — 81
   Communication – Bridges, Walls, and the Path to Health
9. Day 9 — 91
   Energy – Where Do You Find It, and How Do You Use It?
10. Day 10 — 99
    The Brain – The Power Station That Governs Our Lives
11. Day 11 — 107
    The Journey – Growing, Learning and Evolving
12. Day 12 — 117
    Are you a Prisoner?
13. Day 13 — 125
    Embracing What Is – You Don't Know What You've Got Until It's Gone
14. Day 14 — 133
    Habits and Lifestyle Development The Path to Balance and Well-Being

15. Day 15   143
Neurotransmitters – How We Shape Our Well-being

16. Day 16   155
Understanding the World Better – The Value of Reading and Inner Peace

17. Day 17   163
The Judge – A Journey to Compassion and Self-Understanding

18. Day 18   171
Active with Yourself" – The Journey from Co-dependence to Self-Respect

19. Day 19   183
Core Values – The Foundation of Well-being and Decisions

20. Day 20   191
The Body – The Foundation of Well-Being and Balance

21. Day 21   201
The Being – The Journey of Inner Growth and Self-Discovery

22. Day 22   211
The Cost of Inaction – Breaking Free from Limiting Patterns

23. Day 23   221
To Love and Be Loved

24. Day 24   229
Addiction – Understanding Its Roots and Transforming Its Drive

25. Day 25   241
Work – The Process and the Rewards

26. Day 26   247
The Toolbox for a Better Life – Cultivating Lifestyle Through Conscious Habits and Tools

27. Notes and References   263

Introduction

Awakening Awareness

A Travel Guide to the Labyrinth of Existence

How will you change if you consistently apply your knowledge? While many people try to appear knowledgeable or present themselves well, my experience shows that they often prioritize sharing what they already know over gaining new insights. Yet, true growth requires humility, curiosity, and an open mind.

This book is an exploration of how to discover what lies within you and reshape your journey toward fulfillment and freedom.

Core Concepts

Simplicity is the Key to Success

- Meeting your needs in simple ways creates peace in your heart.

- Avoid unnecessary burdens: instead of filling a bucket, ignite the fire within you—the fire of change and creation.

Attention and Intention are the Keys

- Focus and examination generate new energy.
- Whatever you give attention to becomes more significant.
- By doing your best, you find inner peace—and that's what truly matters.
- Chase your dreams, or risk giving nightmares space to grow.

The Nature of Habits

- *Bad habits* offer instant gratification but come at a cost.
- *Good habits* require investment and effort but yield long-term rewards.
- True healing comes from addressing the root, not just tinkering with the branches.

Breaking Patterns

Most people struggle to break patterns sewn into them by life and circumstances. Over time, they tighten those patterns themselves.

- The longer you wait, the more it hurts.

- Open the gate and close the gap between where you are and where you want to be.

Life's Questions

- What does a window of change often open to during a lifetime?
- Does anything change until thought or conversation changes?
- Which is better: a monologue or a dialogue?
- Why are we meddling with remote controls that belong to others?
- How does one earn a promotion?
- Are satisfied needs motivating?
- Is the world a wolf in sheep's clothing?
- Which would you prefer: information or experiences?
- Would you rather be a witness or a director?
- What does a poorly oriented person do to their environment?
- What do you need to be able to hold yourself accountable?
- What do you value most in others?
- Do I find resourceful and knowledgeable individuals to be welcome company?
- Have you managed to finish the self-help books you've bought?
- What does the thing you abuse do to you?
- Why prepare yourself mentally?
- What can shame not tolerate?
- What is the cost of foolish advice or questions?

Reflection on Life: Navigating Challenges and Self-Awareness

Life often challenges us to balance doing our best and accepting the worst. When I strive to give my best effort, I find that I am more resilient in facing difficulties. But when anxiety about others takes over, it can spill into my interactions, leading me to project that unease onto those around me.

I start interfering in things that aren't mine to control, a behavior that stems from misplaced energy. This way of living—focused outward rather than inward—is neither fulfilling nor sustainable.

The wisdom of the AA book resonates deeply with me: "Self-examination in solitude is useless." True growth comes not from isolated introspection but from engaging with others.

When I share my thoughts and actions with people who hold me accountable, my inner monologue transforms into a meaningful dialogue. Spiritual practices, too, play a vital role in reducing loneliness; they remind me of the interconnectedness of all things. Writing morning pages is another profound tool—it awakens the creative spirit within me, turning reflection into expression.

Still, life has taught me harsh lessons about the consequences of neglect and abuse—whether of habits, relationships, or substances. These choices often return to me like a boomerang, carrying the impact of their consequences.

When I desire change, I often encounter resistance from within—a part of me, like a stubborn Lazarus, clings to the familiar, even as I yearn for transformation. The window of change is there, but I hesitate, held back by my own reluctance to act.

I've learned that preparation is everything. The actions I take before life's inevitable blows can determine how well I handle them. Mental and emotional readiness become the foundation for resilience. When I avoid shining a light on my shame—when I keep it hidden—it festers, driving me toward self-destructive behaviors.

Reflecting openly on my struggles is essential, even if it feels uncomfortable.

I've also realized that honesty in relationships is a double-edged sword. I once told a friend that people were saying he was still dealing drugs. He hasn't spoken to me since.

On another occasion, I met a friend who was divorced and neglecting his child. I told him to pull himself together and take responsibility for his life. He, too, stopped speaking to me.

These experiences make me question: when does honesty help, and when does it harm? Am I offering my truth in a way that invites growth, or am I inadvertently pushing people away?

Practical Guidance for Growth

Obstacles and Change

- The "old man" within us is like gravity, constantly pulling us back into old habits.

- Change requires effort, determination, and a willingness to take the first steps, no matter how challenging.

- Without clear direction and intention, 95% of changes may revert to old patterns.

Ignorance and Its Impact

- Ignorance often causes fear and suffering. Understanding the process of life removes much of this fear.

- When life is seen in context, the bigger picture provides clarity and reduces anxiety.

- Success depends on knowing how to reach your goals; without this understanding, we remain stuck.

Energy and Communication

- Surrounding yourself with unsettling energy shortens your temper and drains your emotional reserves.

- Effective communication starts with grounding yourself and engaging with others from a place of balance.

The Subconscious and Truth

- The subconscious resists change and clings to familiarity, even when it's not beneficial.

- This resistance often manifests as projections or overreactions in behavior.

- Coaching can help align your inner compass and guide you toward a path of less resistance and greater satisfaction.

———

Daily Practices for Change - Daily Intentions

- Count how many temptations you resist each day.
- Focus on nourishing, not depleting, yourself.

Starting Healthy Habits - If you struggle to exercise:

1. Prepare your workout clothes the night before.
2. Wake up, put on your gear, grab coffee, and head out.
3. Listen to motivating music and avoid overthinking—just get started.

Reflection Questions

- Are your habits contributing to your growth or hindering it?
- Are you prioritizing short-term gratification over long-term fulfillment?

Wisdom for Transformation - Foundations for Growth

- Trust the structures you've built in your life to withstand challenges.
- Reduce what numbs you and increase what moves you toward vitality.
- Transformation requires follow-through and a deep understanding of the process.

―――

Healing Through Awareness

- Healing begins with understanding: where preparation meets opportunity, growth occurs.

- Experience provides grounding, but repetition is stronger than experience.

The Spiritual Aspect

- Everything we do is spiritual preparation for the next stage of life.

- Align your actions with values that nurture and elevate you.

Final Reflections

Transformation begins when the conversation changes. Will you choose to enforce discipline and self-control, or will you focus on calming your nervous system and finding balance through intentional practices like meditation and nature?

Would you rather count calories and constantly restrict yourself, or move with purpose and joy?
    The choice is yours: to live reactively or to navigate the labyrinth of existence with clarity, simplicity, and intention.

There Is So Much you know that You Don't Know
Until You Do, If You're Lucky

This was the working title for this book. Why? Because it has been the story of my life. When this journey began, I had such a long way to go, but I have been incredibly fortunate.

Albert Einstein once said that what made him remarkable was his curiosity. For me, curiosity has been a necessity—to save my life and then to truly live it.

I've cultivated a deep curiosity about people and myself. It has broadened my perspective and granted me a comforting sense of space within my existence.

Instructions

This book is a workshop! Take a moment to reflect both before and after reading each chapter. This will help quiet the noise and enhance your ability to absorb awareness. Each chapter is packed with content, so read only one chapter per day.

Pay attention!

<u>What's most important on this journey: After answering the questions with long, well-thought-out responses, read your answers aloud and have someone you trust listen to you.</u>

It can be very helpful to work through this process with a partner.

Day 1

Execution is the Motivation

T his first chapter underscores the transformative power of action, emphasizing that steady execution of small, intentional steps fosters self-discipline, inner peace, and long-term well-being.

Take a deep breath and meditate for 5 minutes

The Compass and the First Step

Execution is like setting a compass to true north and taking the first step toward your destination. The compass represents your intention—your vision of where you want to go.

However, it's the first step, no matter how small, that turns direction into action. Each step builds momentum, transforming potential energy into a journey of self-discipline, fulfillment, and growth.

My Story: Developing New Software

In 2004, I decided to attend a meditation course. I had long intended to start meditating but never managed to begin. The course was expensive, but the returns were immeasurable. 🙂

The course taught us to meditate for 20 minutes on an empty stomach in the morning and again in the afternoon. For me, someone who had always struggled to stand firm and break old habits, this was a significant step.

Gradually, I began making better decisions. This became one of the best times of my life. I had set goals before, time and again, but rarely achieved them. Meditation changed that. It opened the back door to my subconscious and helped me take better care of myself—effortlessly.

During this time, I lost a significant amount of weight, which became a running joke with my friend Binni, who constantly had to punch new holes in my belt as it got smaller day by day. This transformation wasn't just physical; it was a mental shift that profoundly impacted my life.

Transformative Elements

To Create Effective Execution

- Assess your skills and challenges, aiming for balance—don't stretch the bowstring too tight.
- Procrastination makes today easy but tomorrow hard. Start executing now so it doesn't weigh on you.
- Say no to quick fixes and become the rock on which your success is built.
- Tomorrow doesn't exist—stop planning and stalling; start starting and stop stopping.

As Proverbs 19:8 says: *"To acquire wisdom is to love yourself; people who cherish understanding will prosper."*

Key Thoughts on Growth

- Don't give up—don't yield to bad habits.
- Overcoming your weaknesses makes you extraordinary in your own eyes.
- When you conquer the mind, you conquer yourself—and that is life's ultimate victory.
- Your self-esteem grows with purposeful execution.

Execution is the Motivation! As Aristotle said:
   "The purpose of knowledge is action,
   not knowledge."

Stress Comes from Lack of Control
"More stress calls for more organization." This isn't just about filling ourselves with more information but igniting passion.

Execution stems from resolve and balance, not chaos. Reaching a point where we do less of what we "need" and more of what we "want" is the key to joy and success.

Ask yourself: *What must happen first for me to ... ?*

To build a life with ever-expanding horizons, focus on starting small but with intention.

A seed grows under the pressure of the soil; our physical form reflects our personal growth.

This is the journey of a traveller, embarking with healthy intentions and discovering that strength lies in balance.

The Pit We Fall Into Again and Again
The road to achievement is paved with balance. Despite the best intentions, Friday comes after a hard week, and we think, *"Should we just order pizza?"* Saturday follows, bringing discomfort and revealing imbalance.

The pit we fall into repeatedly is called imbalance—*"too much tension that threatens to burn it all down."*

The body's energy level is the driver. If you care for the home you live in (your body and mind), you are more likely to maintain steady footing on life's climb.

———

Learning to Harness Inner Motivation

Distractions are the biggest enemy of success. They disrupt the brain, destroy focus, and foster disorder.

Purposeful rest and creating balance help the brain function optimally. Simplifying and relaxing bring us closer to our strengths.

Less – More – Stop – Start

We need to regularly ask ourselves what we want:

- *Less:* What in my life drains my energy?
- *More:* What brings me joy and strengthens me?
- *Stop:* What habit or behavior could I stop that no longer serves me?
- *Start:* What new habit could I adopt to support my growth?

Strengthening Willpower and Taking Action

- Willpower is like a muscle—it grows with practice. In what areas of your life can you improve it?

- Action matters. Only the present moment counts.

Key Phrases for Execution:

- When I remember, I act.
- When I see, I act.
- What I can't do now, I note for later action.

A Real-Life Story: Baby Steps

Stella lost 65 kg after making small, sustainable changes. As she began to see results, her excitement grew, and she was motivated to do even more!

A Real-Life Story: The First Step to Execution

Anna spent years in a cycle of knowing what to do but not acting. She knew she needed to exercise, eat healthier, and prioritize her well-being, but each day ended with the words: *"I'll start tomorrow."* Her closet was full of clothes that no longer fit, and every morning began with self-criticism in front of the mirror.

One day, Anna decided enough was enough. She wrote a single sentence on a piece of paper: *"Start starting and stop stopping."*

She began small setting her alarm 10 minutes earlier and meditating briefly in the mornings.

The following week, she added a 15-minute walk.

Gradually, she shifted her focus from imagining monumental changes to celebrating small steps.

After a few months, Anna felt lighter—not just physically but mentally. Her self-criticism diminished as her actions aligned with her intentions.

Her greatest victory wasn't fitting into her old clothes or decluttering her closet but regaining the confidence that came from executing what she knew she needed to do.

Life Is Behavior in Search of well-being

Our behavioral patterns are rooted in the subconscious.

We often overestimate short-term impacts and underestimate long-term effects.

Bad habits offer instant gratification, while good habits require perseverance and patience, paid in steady installments. "Well-being comes from within."

Practical Tips for Execution

1. *What would nourish me to implement today?*
2. Example: Drink more water, eat fresh vegetables, meditate, or go to bed earlier.
3. *Peace begins with steady, intentional execution:*
4. Take things slowly and avoid overwhelming yourself.
5. *Focus on presence and purpose in daily life:*

Observe your habits, reflect on them, and find ways to improve.

Example Plans: "I want to be more present and better at noticing what is here and now."

- "I want to create a peaceful environment for my family by starting with self-care."

Plan

- Meditate for 10 minutes in the morning or journal thoughts.
- Dedicate at least one hour a day to physical activity.
- Recharge before coming home—take a walk, swim, or hit the gym.

Self-Reflecting Questions - Healthy Desire

1. What do I enjoy that others might see as work?

2. What activities make me lose track of time and feel in a state of flow?
3. Where do I excel, and how can I better use those skills?
4. What habits or attitudes could help me grow today?

Self-Reflecting Questions – Steps to Grow

1. What small actions can I take today to support the person I want to be?
2. What habits or thoughts have kept me stuck, and how can I let them go?
3. How can I create an environment that fosters growth and peace in my life?

Final Words

"Execution comes from the place where you rest."

As I have been writing this book the self-doubt comes through the backdoor. But every time I start working the doubt goes away and I get filled with trust and confidence.

Slow down and let calm guide your actions. Remember, there is no "later" or "someday"—there is only now. Start starting and stop stopping.

Answer the questions and meditate for 10 minutes. Reflect on what you are sensing after this work and write it down

Day 2

The Mastery League – Living Life Like a Champion

This chapter outlines how to live like a champion by cultivating intentional habits such as mindfulness, movement, healthy eating, meaningful conncctions, and self-discipline to create balance, clarity, and fulfillment in life.

Take a deep breath and meditate for 5 minutes

The Symphony of Mastery

Living life like a champion is akin to conducting a symphony. Each instrument—mindfulness, movement, nutrition, connection, and self-discipline—must play in harmony to create a masterpiece.

The conductor is your intention, guiding each element to contribute its part with balance and clarity. When every note aligns, the result is a life of fulfillment, where every moment resonates with purpose and joy.

Living life like a champion means approaching each moment with awareness, anticipation, and self-discipline. Masters understand their own bodies and minds, striving to develop these qualities through regular self-care, balance, and rest.

Transformative elements

Morning as the Foundation of a Good Day

The morning is the most precious time of the day; it lays the foundation for how the day unfolds.

Mindfulness in your morning routine creates calm, focus, and the expectation of a constructive day.

Consider this question: *"What does my morning routine look like, and how can it strengthen me?"*

Ways to Set the Foundation for a Good Day

- Wake up earlier by establishing intentional sleep habits.
- Start your day with water, meditation, and writing (morning pages).
- Prepare nutritious meals for yourself and your loved ones.
- Practice mindfulness – greet people with a smile and their name.

Meditation is like a fast for the mind; it rests the brain, enhancing your ability to make sound decisions. The brain – the most energy-consuming organ in your body – rewards you with increased awareness, calm, and clarity when given proper rest.

Exercise and Outdoor Activities

Exercise is the key to physical and mental balance. Find movement you enjoy and that brings you joy. Being outdoors provides fresh oxygen, which is especially crucial during the dark and cold winter months.

Ways to Incorporate Movement and Outdoor Time

- Walks in nature.
- Hiking, walking, Cross-country skiing or swimming.
- Activities that delight you, such as yoga, running, or cycling.

Oxygen is essential for physical and mental well-being. It nourishes us and connects us to nature.

Fasting and Nutrition – breakfast means break the fast!
Fasting is like meditation for the body; it gives it the quiet it needs to cleanse and rejuvenate. Intermittent fasting, such as from 6:00 PM to 9:00 AM, can positively impact energy and physical balance. Avoid white flour, yeast, and sugar to stabilize appetite and sustain energy.

Examples of Healthy Eating and Fasting Practices

- Drink water when you wake up to help the body cleanse itself.
- Eat whole, living foods that support energy and well-being.
- Give your body breaks to rest your digestive system.

Discovering Healthy Desires
Healthy desires are the foundation of personal growth and well-being. They help us shape a clear vision for life and give us direction to pursue what truly matters.

Three Steps to Cultivate Healthy Desires

1. *Identify Healthy Desires*

Ask yourself: *What do I truly want? What desires serve my health, well-being, and happiness?* Healthy desires strengthen both your body and mind.

2. *Plant Seeds That Support Your Desires*

Once you've defined your desires, lay the groundwork with consistent, intentional actions that support them. Small, mindful steps act as seeds that grow toward your goal.

3. *The Constant Ripple*

Repeat your desire in your mind regularly, like a constant ripple. Remind yourself of your purpose through positive affirmations and clear direction. This helps maintain focus and drive.

Examples of Healthy Desires in Action:

Example 1: Being Present and Perceiving What Truly Matters.

Healthy Desire - I want to be more present in the moment and perceive what truly matters. *Seeds to Plant:*

- Quiet the mind with morning meditation.
- Prioritize quality sleep and nutritious eating.
- Move for at least 1 hour daily through walking, yoga, or running.
- Rejuvenate the body with daily sauna and cold plunges.
- Think less and experience more by practicing mindfulness and attention.

Example 2: Giving My Best to Those Who Matter Most:

. . .

Healthy Desire - I want to return home at my best, bringing nourishment to my closest relationships. *Seeds to Plant:*

- Before coming home from work, recharge with a walk or gym session.
- If time is tight, create a shared experience by doing something together.
- Focus on positive thoughts and self-care during your commute to bring uplifting energy into your home.

Reflections

Healthy desires are the cornerstone of life quality. When we discover what we truly want and support it with intentional actions, life blossoms. By repeating these desires in our minds, we strengthen our resolve to follow through. *What healthy desire will you introduce today?*

Daily Practices for Positivity and Productivity: Find Daily Anticipation: Set a clear intention for your day to make it unique and seize the opportunity.

Examples:

1. Try to make everyone you meet smile.
2. Be fully present and listen without planning your response. Offer your undivided attention.
3. Consume only energizing calories. Before eating, ask yourself: *Will this give me energy or take it away?*
4. Take intentional breaks—go for a walk, listen to calming music, read something uplifting, and recharge before returning home to give your best.
5. Aim for 10,000 steps a day.

6. Arrive at work refreshed, do everything required with joy, and go beyond expectations where possible.
7. Address imbalances—pick up trash, uplift someone feeling low, or help restore harmony when you see something out of sync.
8. Find your own 😊

Fostering Meaningful Connections

Belonging is one of the richest needs under the sun. Healthy connections with others are invaluable. Playing board games, walking together, or sharing heartfelt conversations creates deep bonds.

Ideas for Strengthening Connections

- Spend quality time with friends and family.
- Cultivate relationships with people who lift you up.
- Listen sincerely and show presence in your interactions.

Core Elements of Well-Being

1. Relationships and Belonging: Human connections form the foundation of life satisfaction.
2. Intentional Movement: Choose activities that are enjoyable and nourishing.
3. Good Sleep: The bedrock of balance and well-being.
4. Meditation: Quiet the mind to improve clarity and calm.
5. Oxygen and Nature: Outdoor time strengthens both body and mind.
6. Healthy Connections: Share your heart and deepen relationships.

7. Eating Living Foods: Opt for energy-boosting, nutritious meals.
8. Spiritual Growth with Others: Foster personal and collective development.
9. Intentional Rest: Make time for renewal.
10. Cold Baths and Saunas: Excellent for improving sleep and well-being.
11. Grounding: Walk barefoot on grass or engage in open water swimming.
12. Becoming Part of Nature: Regularly immerse yourself in its effects.

A Real-Life Story

Jonas wanted to improve his lifestyle and live as a "master" in his own life. He started waking up earlier, drinking water, and meditating in the mornings. He improved his diet and incorporated outdoor walks and exercise.

With these changes, Jonas found greater calm and focus in his daily life, enabling him to face challenges and savor the good moments each day offered.

Self-Reflecting Questions

1. What simple actions can you take today to live like a champion and improve your quality of life?
2. Who do you want to bring along on your journey to live consciously and well?
3. How do you want these lifestyle changes to impact your health, relationships, and well-being?

Final Words

The mastery league isn't about perfection but about balance and growth. Will you choose to meditate and calm your system or push through with sheer willpower? Are you willing to move as much as possible or closely monitor your diet?

Answer the questions and meditate for 10 minutes. Reflect on what you are sensing after this work and write it down

Day 3

Time – Slowing Down, Savoring, and Harnessing Life's Most Precious Resource

This Chapter explores the profound impact of mindful time management, emphasizing the importance of living in the present, reducing distractions, and embracing intentional routines to transform time into a tool for growth, balance, and fulfillment.

Take a deep breath and meditate for 5 minutes

The Hourglass in the Wind

Time is like an hourglass resting in the wind. The sand flows steadily, grain by grain, representing the precious moments of life. While we can't stop the flow, we can shield the hourglass from the gusts of distraction, letting each grain fall with purpose.

When we embrace the present, we witness the beauty of each passing moment, transforming time from something fleeting into something deeply cherished.

Time is like a river - You cannot touch the same water twice because the flow that has passed will never pass again. Make it count".

Time is not merely a measure of life but a priceless tool for growth, learning, and inner peace. In today's fast-paced world, many of us feel pressed for time, but with mindful practices, we can transform time from a source of pressure into an ally.

By slowing down and approaching time with purpose, we unlock balance, satisfaction, and a deeper connection to life.

We All Have Watches, But No Time!

"If you don't decide how to spend your time, someone else will decide for you."

This sentiment rings true for many. We hear phrases like:

- "It's always Friday."
- "Christmas is here again already."
- "I never have time for myself."

The feeling that time is slipping away reflects not just the speed of our surroundings but also how we choose to spend it. Without direction, time controls us. But with intentional decisions, we can make time work in our favor.

Being Enough – Letting Go of Conditions and Living in the Present
I've often been haunted by the feeling of not being enough—as if who I am now isn't deserving of happiness, success, or love. There's always that inner voice whispering, "You need to achieve this first."

- I've told myself, *"I can't approach my boss until I have everything figured out."*
- Yet, while time ticks by, the windows of opportunity close, not because I lack desire, but because I always postpone things for a "better time" that never comes.

My Story: My Eyes Opened

For two years, I admired a woman I was deeply drawn to. She had a radiant smile that warmed me every time she saw me.

I knew I was captivated. But instead of stepping forward, I told myself I needed to be better—more worthy.

Years passed, and as I sensed her growing distant, she finally said: *"I care about you deeply."* Her words were both beautiful and heartbreaking.

She had felt the same way all along, but my fear of not being enough had held me back from acting.

Lessons learned

- Time doesn't wait. You don't need to be better, richer, or more prepared to deserve life.
- Courage is living now. Stepping forward despite insecurities is how you win.

This experience taught me the value of being present in life and ceasing to wait for a moment when I feel "enough." The truth is: I am enough, right now.

Transformative Elements

Time – A Guiding Light for Better Living

Time is a precious resource. How we use it affects our well-being and quality of life.

Managed well, it fosters growth and balance. Mismanaged, it leads to stress and anxiety.

Understanding Time

- *"The purpose of time is to empower you to use it constructively."*
- When time isn't utilized for growth and learning, it loses its meaning.
- Speed can diminish wisdom; slowing down allows us to maximize time's potential.
- Poor time management creates discomfort, a loss of control, and heightened anxiety.

Ways to Slow Down and Use Time Wisely:

1. *Focus on the Present*

Being fully present reduces stress and enhances joy. Concentrating on one task at a time simplifies and enriches life.

2. *Reduce Unnecessary Distractions*

Devices like phones, computers, and TVs can drain time and energy. Setting boundaries with these tools allows the mind to recharge.

3. *Intentional Planning*

Prioritize tasks that align with your values and goals. Consciously choose to invest in what truly matters to you.

4. *Embrace a Calm Morning Routine*

Mornings set the tone for the day. Spend time meditating, journaling, or focusing on your priorities.

5. *View Time as an Asset*

Time isn't an obstacle; it's an opportunity to learn, grow, and connect more deeply with yourself and others.

A Real-Life Story: Slowing Down and Rethinking Time

Elisabeth often felt like time was running away from her. Always rushing, she rarely made time for herself. One day, she decided to track how she spent every hour of her week. She realized a large portion of her time was wasted scrolling through her phone and stressing over unfinished tasks.

She decided to slow down and adjust her routine.

- She started her mornings with 10 minutes of meditation.
- She focused on completing one task before moving on to the next.
- She reduced her screen time and spent more moments with her family.

After a few weeks, Elisabeth felt more energized, balanced, and fulfilled.

Self-Reflecting Questions

1. What in your life drains your time and energy?
2. How can you create space to savor the present moment?
3. What habits can you develop to manage your time more wisely?

Final Words

Time – Friend or Foe?

Time is a tool we desire most but often misuse. It becomes our friend when we invest it in what matters and our foe when we let it control us.

We only have one moment at a time—either we overthink it or live it.

Taking charge of our time transforms life into a meaningful and fulfilling journey.

. . .

"Don't wait for the perfect moment—take this moment and make it perfect."

Answer the questions and meditate for 10 minutes. Reflect on what you are sensing after this work and write it down

Day 4

Designing Your Health Box

This fourth chapter explores the importance of creating a "health box"—a balanced environment that nourishes the body and mind—through intentional habits, self-respect, and removing distractions, enabling personal growth and simplicity.

Take a deep breath and meditate for 5 minutes

The Garden of Well-Being

Creating your health box is like cultivating a garden. The soil represents your environment, and the seeds symbolize the habits you plant.

For your garden to thrive, it requires care—removing weeds (distractions and harmful influences), watering consistently (intentional actions), and ensuring sunlight reaches every part (self-respect and positive relationships). With patience and attention, the garden grows into a sanctuary of balance and vitality, reflecting the effort you've invested.

Create Your Own Health Box

In this chapter, you'll learn how to design your life in a simple and constructive way.

If I could travel 30 years back in time and give myself advice, it would be this: Design your own health box.

Life is about balance and creating an environment that supports the needs of your body and mind. What we put into our bodies reflects how we feel, just as the mind produces what it has been trained to think.

. . .

Environment is critical for development!

Businesspeople often say, "Location, location, location." But I say, "Environment, environment, environment." If you want an extraordinary life, it begins with creating an environment that nourishes and empowers you.

Men especially love the concept of a "nothing box"—keeping life simple and selectively choosing what to allow in. Breaking unhelpful patterns and designing new ones can create transformative change. When fear of change takes the wheel, fear becomes the captain of your life.

My Story

> *"Simplicity is so obviously one of the characteristics of truth that it is sometimes confused with it."* – Joseph Joubert

In 2014, I attended a workshop that I didn't expect to change my life. We started by sitting in a circle and introducing ourselves. Then, we were given a task: to repeatedly say, "I really want to…"

As we repeated this sentence, the discomfort gradually faded, and something inside me began to release. Later, we created vision boards, danced, and connected with ourselves. Finally, we sat back in the circle to complete the same sentence, this time from our hearts.

I closed my eyes, took a deep breath, and said from deep within: "I really want to simplify my life."

This surprised me. I hadn't realized my life was complicated. I didn't know simplicity was something I craved. But there I was, holding this unexpected awareness.

Transformative Elements

Steps to Create Your Health Box

. . .

1. Self-Reflection and Energy Choices

As King Solomon said in Proverbs:
"Avoid bad company."

- Choosing the right people to surround yourself with starts with being a good companion to yourself.

- We all have tolerance systems that can endure tough situations for a time, but when our "pain tank" fills, we are forced to make changes.

- Pain is a sign we must learn to listen to if we want to grow.

2. The Power of Words and Self-Respect

- Use constructive words that strengthen your self-respect.

- Say "I don't want to" instead of "I can't." This shows resolve and strength.

- Your words are your personal brand and reflect the lifestyle you aim to create. Showing yourself, respect, warmth, and admiration is the foundation of balance and well-being.

3. Key Elements of the Health Box

- *Sleep:* Use sleep to renew your body and mind.

- *Exercise:* Choose activities that bring joy and strengthen your body.

- *Nutrition:* Eat foods that promote balance and happiness.

- *Relationships:* Surround yourself with people who uplift and empower you.

- *Meditation:* Take time to quiet your mind and reset.

4. *Avoid Distractions*

- Remove anything that drains your energy, whether it's negative influences from your environment, clutter, or toxic relationships.

5. *Cultivate Peace*

- Peace is a game-changer. Disruption robs you of control and paralyzes your being. Choose to nourish what brings inner calm and strength.

The Evolution of Health and Balance

I have worked as a personal coach for 22 years in a large fitness center with a diverse group of people. A noticeable pattern emerges among those who come at similar times of the day.

- *4% are consistently in top shape*

These are individuals who were essentially "gifted" with a healthy foundation early on.

Most have been exercising regularly—more than 10 hours a week—since a young age and have built a lifestyle to support their fitness.

- *25% are in good shape*

This group maintains balance and achieves results, but they need to put in consistent effort to stay there.

- *The majority struggles to maintain balance*

This group often finds themselves battling to establish equilibrium, breaking free from old patterns that were ingrained in them early in life.
Over time, they must actively work on creating better habits and routines.

Time and the Gap

The longer you wait to break these patterns, the harder it becomes. Over time, the gap between your current state and the goals you aspire to grows wider. Open the gate and close the gap. You can start the process now—*it's never too late to take the first steps.*

Facing Distortions

Nothing has as many lives as a distortion you refuse to correct. Corrections can be painful and require courage, but they are essential to finding balance and harmony.

Many people surround themselves with others who have stopped pointing out the changes they need to make. When the well of corrections dries up, it's often time to pause and reevaluate.

If you're in the wrong place in life, it can be difficult to see your true worth. We often choose what's familiar, not necessarily what's good for us. The subconscious plays a big role—it pulls us back into old patterns that align with learned behaviors. Changing this requires awareness and determination.

Reflections on Growth and Change

- *You overthink because you don't write things down.* Writing is a release valve for the mind. When thoughts overflow, writing puts them in order.
- *You feel anxious because you don't take action.* Anxiety thrives on inaction. Taking even the smallest step turns fear into progress.
- *You procrastinate because you don't have a plan.* A clear plan turns overwhelming tasks into actionable steps. Without one, uncertainty takes over.
- *You feel stressed because you don't train.* Physical and mental training builds resilience against life's pressures.
- *You lack clarity because you don't keep a journal.* Journaling provides perspective. It breaks confusion into clarity.

One reason people resist change is because they focus on what they have to give up instead of what they stand to gain.

Shifting the narrative transforms fear into opportunity. Growth happens when you embrace what lies ahead instead of clinging to what holds you back.

Every habit, action, and perspective we choose can either keep us stuck or propel us forward. Small changes lead to significant transformations.

Steps Toward ChangeFind Emotional Leverage

Ask yourself, what ignites me? How can I use this to move forward?

1. *Identify the Source of Answers*

Listen to your intuition and distinguish true needs from noise and clutter.

  2. *Let the Noise Fade*

When you tune into your inner needs, distractions diminish, and clarity emerges.

  3. *Take Action*

Once you face your tasks, procrastination gives way to courage.

Self-Reflecting Questions

1. Which aspects of your life support your well-being, and which ones harm it?

2. What distortions in your life are you avoiding correcting, and how can you address them?

3. How can you change your environment to improve your well-being and strengthen your self-respect?

Final Words – Living Consciously

Designing your health box is the greatest gift you can give yourself.

With awareness and intention, you can create a life that balances and aligns with both your body and mind.

By prioritizing sleep, nutrition, exercise, relationships, and peace, life transforms.

Answer the questions and meditate for 10 minutes. Reflect on what you are sensing after this work and write it down

Day 5

The Mind – Enhancing Awareness and Mastering Your Thoughts

Chapter five emphasizes the power of mastering thoughts by breaking old patterns, practicing mindfulness, and creating new mental habits that foster presence, balance, and personal growth.

Take a deep breath and meditate for 5 minutes

The Sculptor and the Marble

The mind is like a block of marble, full of potential but shaped by its surroundings and experiences. Each thought is a chisel strike—some refine the form, while others create cracks.

A mindful sculptor chooses each strike with intention, shaping the marble into a masterpiece. By mastering your thoughts, you become the artist of your mind, crafting a work of balance, presence, and growth.

Thoughts as Obstacles or Solutions: "A new level of thinking."

"The significant problems we face cannot be solved at the same level of thinking we were at when we created them."
    – Albert Einstein.

The mind is the control center where everything begins and ends. It has the power to lift us up or pull us down. If you don't control your mind, your mind will control you. Thoughts can be like old connections that need to be unplugged. Nothing changes until thinking changes.

We always have just one moment – we are either thinking or experiencing. By practicing how to experience rather than constantly chase after information, we open doors to freedom and calm. When the mind shifts between the past and the future, we miss the present moment, where life truly happens.

My Story

Between the ages of 17 and 22, I set the same goals every summer before attending a big outdoor festival.

I wanted to look good and meet a girl. Every year, I made this decision with determination, hoping it would somehow happen.

But I changed nothing – I just desperately tried to starve myself. Meanwhile, I kept drinking every weekend and couldn't understand why I never reached my goals.

The Old Self – The Gravity That Holds Us Back

The "old self," that part of us stuck in habits and patterns, acts like gravity. It pulls us down repeatedly, even when we decide to aim for new goals.

To break through this gravity and achieve real change, we must do more than decide – we must roll up our sleeves, step into discomfort, and make true changes.

The Process of Change

Research shows that 95% of changes we attempt fall into an automatic "backward gear."

Our old patterns take over unless we consciously work to break them. *What I Learned From These Years:*

1. *Intentions Alone Are Not Enough*

Deciding on something without changing the lifestyle or habits holding you back is destined to fail.

2. *Change Requires Systems*

It's not enough to just try avoiding certain temptations or starving yourself. You must create an environment and conditions that support the change.

3. *The Old Self Won't Let Go Easily*

Breaking free requires both willpower and a plan.

Questions for You:

- What old habit or mindset has been holding you back?
- What can you do today to roll up your sleeves and start making real change?

Transformative elements

The Power of Thoughts and Their Impact on Our Lives
Our thoughts aren't just words passing through the mind – they have the power to shape our emotions, behaviors, and even future.

When we let the mind produce constant worries and unnecessary demands, it creates anxiety and tension that disconnect us from the present.

We enter a "needy" state where the mind takes control, often cheered on by fear and insecurity. This can prevent us from living in alignment with our true values and desires.

Learning to Step Out of the Cycle

1. *The Mind as a Room*

Imagine the mind as a room where all your habitual ideas about life are stored.

These ideas have become part of your unconscious responses.

By realizing that you have control over this room, you can choose to open the doors or clean it out.

2. *Say "STOP"*

When you notice your mind wandering, tell yourself "STOP." This is a mental switch that helps reconnect you to the present moment. You can even create a physical reminder, like lightly tapping your chest, to bring yourself back.

3. *Are You Thinking or Experiencing?*

Regularly ask yourself: "Am I thinking or experiencing?" This simple question can help you identify whether you're caught in mental chatter or connected to reality. When you're experiencing, you're present – you feel, sense, and live in the moment.

Ways to Harness the Power of Thoughts

- *Gratitude:* Train your mind to focus on what is good and fulfilling in your life. This can range from small moments of joy to significant milestones.

- *Neutrality:* Practice observing your thoughts without letting them control you. They aren't the truth, just lively musings of the mind.

- *Action:* When you're aware of negative thoughts, respond with a positive action that aligns with your values and goals.

Challenge for You

The next time you feel your mind taking over, use your mental switch. Return to the present and ask yourself: "Am I thinking or experiencing?" This simple step can transform your day.

The Theater of the Mind:
> *The curtains drawn back, the show begins.*
> *Each in their place, all the information,*
> *Images from every direction,*
> *A living play in many acts.*
> – Eiki Einars

The mind is like a theater constantly presenting new stories, memories, and ideas. This show can be captivating but can also pull us away from reality.

The most important thing we can do is catch unconscious thoughts before they take hold – like stopping a catfish from slipping into your box.

Difficult Thoughts and Experiences

Someone out of balance often struggles to see what's really happening. The mind ends up in a tug-of-war with itself, pulling us away from the present.

When you feel disoriented, it's crucial to open a conversation – call a friend and share what you're experiencing. The longer you wait to share, the harder it becomes.

We often get stuck in thoughts that begin with "when".

- When I get in shape.
- When my partner changes.
- When my boss recognizes my talents.

These thoughts pull us out of the moment and give unnecessary power to external circumstances.

However, the mind can be trained to let go of these "when" thoughts and live in the now.

Exercises to Calm the Mind

1. *The Five-Second Rule:* When a negative thought arises, give yourself five seconds to evaluate it and replace it with a positive thought.

2. *Deep Breathing:* If you feel stressed, take 20 deep breaths, releasing negative thoughts with each exhale.

3. *Unplug Old Connections:* Shine a light on hidden thoughts and ask: "Can I think about this differently?"

4. *Think and Act:* When an uncomfortable feeling arises, find a thought that supports action. For example: "I'm overweight" – drink a glass of water and say, "I'm taking responsibility."

5. *Expression and Flow:* Talk to someone you trust. Sharing thoughts helps release tension and allows the mind to flourish.

The Mind and Self-Identity

We often care more about how we look than how we think and speak. But when we conquer the mind, we conquer ourselves – and that is life's greatest victory.

By putting life into a healthy perspective, fear loses its power.

. . .

Life in the Moment

Life happens only now. When the mind creates limitations with thoughts like, "When I become…," we miss what truly matters.

Practice seeing the bigger picture and ask: "What is really happening now?"

Creating New Habits

Thoughts are like seeds growing in the soil of the mind. If you remove mental clutter, thoughts can grow in a direction that fosters growth.

By creating new mental pathways, removing limitations, and practicing regularly, you can form habits that transform your life.

A Real-Life Story: Letting Go of Old Thoughts

Sara often felt stuck in thoughts about what others thought of her. She would think, "When I become smarter, people will take me seriously." These thoughts controlled her life until she decided to change.

She began practicing the five-second rule. When a negative thought came up, she asked herself: "What can I do about this now?"

Gradually, she shifted her focus to what she could control, like showing herself respect in her words and actions.

Over time, her life transformed – she saw the bigger picture and took control of her mind.

Self-Reflecting Questions

1. What thoughts limit you and prevent you from enjoying the present moment?

2. How can you start unplugging the old connections holding you back?
3. How can you practice experiencing more and thinking less?

Final Words – Guiding the Mind

The mind can be our best friend or worst enemy.

By managing our thoughts and creating new mental pathways, we can live in balance and harmony.

When we conquer the mind, we conquer ourselves. What will you do today to start working with your mind?

Answer the questions and meditate for 10 minutes. Reflect on what you are sensing after this work and write it down

Day 6
Knowledge for the Mind, Experience for the Body – Building a New Personality

This chapter explores how self-awareness, facing inner struggles, and creating new experiences can transform old patterns, cultivate inner prosperity, and bring harmony to both mind and body.

Take a deep breath and meditate for 5 minutes

The Potter and the Clay

Transforming your personality is like being a potter shaping clay. The mind represents the knowledge—the vision of the form you wish to create—and the body represents the clay, molded by experiences and actions.

With each touch of intention, the clay takes on new shapes, smoothing old imperfections and forming something stronger and more refined. The potter knows that patience, persistence, and balance between thought and action are key to creating a masterpiece.

Is your personal reality controlling your personality?

Success is fulfilling your needs in a simple way. Life offers countless opportunities to taste new experiences, like free samples in stores. When you find something that makes you feel better, those experiences can change everything.

Understanding the Inner Struggle

It's common to hear people say, "There's so much noise," pointing fingers at external culprits. But what about inner noise?

How do you respond when faced with uncomfortable emotions? When shame, sadness, or boredom arise, what do you do?
Ask yourself:

- Where do these emotions come from?
- What resides within me that triggers them?
- How can my connection with myself help me respond?

Inner peace doesn't come automatically—it requires practice and awareness. Time depends on where we are in our life journey, but our relationship with ourselves is always the cornerstone of well-being.

Transformative elements

Orphaned Energy

During World War I, pregnant women endured great hunger. The children born during this time became food addicts—when they finally had access to food, they couldn't stop eating.

Similarly, children deprived of connection and love experience an inner disconnection. This attachment disruption creates a longing to be loved. Yet, when love eventually arrives, there is no foundation to sustain it, and they end up sabotaging the very thing they desired most.

True Security and Inner Growth

1. Security and Pain

True security doesn't lie in stillness or stagnation but in growth, improvement, and change.

. . .

Pain, which we often try to dull or escape, is actually a gift—it informs us that something is not right. It calls us to re-evaluate, to examine our lives, and to ask: What truly matters?

Instead of numbing the pain, dig deeper for insight. By facing and understanding it, we can grow and strengthen.

Just as the body learns to endure greater physical strain through exercise, we develop mentally by learning to tolerate discomfort.

2. *Thoughts and Limitations*

Our thoughts can act like old connections that keep us tied to unhelpful patterns.

To grow, we must disconnect from these patterns and identify the triggers that pull us backward.

Take responsibility, recognize your limitations, and let them dissolve through acknowledgment and a willingness to change.

3. *Opportunity for Transformation*

The discomfort barrier we imagine is often just a shadow in our minds. When we allow ourselves to see pain as an opportunity for re-evaluation, we start understanding what truly matters.

4. *Cultivating Inner Prosperity*

- *Prosperity comes from within:* It doesn't arise from controlling external circumstances but from how we approach ourselves.

- *Miracles are inner work:* The person who learns to master themselves is the one who masters life.

- *Your inner harmony resides in silence:* Allow yourself to listen to what lies within, free from external noise.

- *Sustainable growth requires roots:* To grow steadily, we need a strong foundation. Self-awareness, responsibility, and a clear vision.

5. Shifts in Values and Lifestyles

Modern times have drastically altered our values and lifestyles through speed, video games, and passive consumption. If we neglect what truly matters—our minds and bodies—we pay the price with anxiety, low energy, and a lack of purpose.

A Real-Life Story

Rut was socially isolated and had a small support network. She often said she didn't know what could help her.

I invited her to join me at a gathering where people shared their experiences and learned to grow. She responded, "This isn't for me." Rut remained in her isolation, stuck in patterns shaped by her past experiences.

> Mother Teresa once said: *"It is not hunger but loneliness that is killing this world."*

Here Lie...

- Unacknowledged emotions that were never brought to light.
- Unspoken words that deserved to be heard.
- Thoughts that never flourished into creativity.
- People you could have known and connected with deeply.
- Unused potentials that never became reality.
- Dreams locked away due to fear or insecurity.
- Ideas that never grew wings to fly.
- Words you should have said, and those you chose not to.

- All the "I should haves" that never became "I did."

Now is the time to uncover, unwind, and allow these things to live. *Change – Fear and Opportunity*

We often have a strong tendency to fear change. Misconceptions can be so deeply rooted that we prefer stagnation over taking steps forward.

But when we let go of this fear, a window opens in the present—a window to try new paths, let old misconceptions fade, and discover fresh opportunities.

"We'd rather destroy ourselves than change," but it is through change that life truly awaits.

Designing Experiences and Schedules

To break free from old patterns, it's essential to create an "experience schedule". Here are some examples:

- *Monday:* Zumba
- *Tuesday:* Weightlifting
- *Wednesday:* Hiking
- *Thursday:* Spinning
- *Friday:* Badminton
- *Saturday:* Weightlifting
- *Sunday:* Rest and spiritual practice

Self-Reflecting Questions

- Who is my best workout partner?
- What is the best exercise that makes me feel good?

The Process of Change – From Skepticism to Preparation. Breaking habits requires you to follow-through

1. Commit to trying new approaches.
2. Adopt new efforts and learn from the experience.
3. Shift from skepticism to preparation and practice.

Knowledge for the Mind, Experience for the Body:
Embracing health often begins with small steps that lead to significant benefits. Joyful, motivating exercise is one of the most powerful tools for improving how we feel.

"There is no someday or one day—there is only NOW."

Ask Yourself:

1. What would be beneficial to implement now?
2. What is the main source of stress in my life right now?
3. We have an innate drive to maintain what we have. What do we want to let go of?

Final Words

New personal experiences bring new dimensions to your personality. Change begins with self-awareness and a willingness to meet yourself where you are.

With courage and consistent effort, you can create inner peace and strength, equipping yourself to face any challenge.

"This isn't just about being kind to myself", this could be the first step toward a new, self-empowered life.

Answer the questions and meditate for 10 minutes. Reflect on what you are sensing after this work and write it down

Day 7

The 5% Syndrome – Upgrading the Mind's Operating System

I n this chapter we dive into the concept of our internal "operating system," revealing how outdated habits and recurring thought patterns consume 95% of our mental energy and provides actionable steps to redesign this system for a more conscious, balanced, and fulfilling life.

Taka a deep breath and meditate for 5 minutes

The Architect and the Blueprint
Our internal operating system is like a blueprint for a house. Over time, the original design becomes outdated—walls crumble, and rooms no longer suit our needs. The architect, our awareness, must step in to revise the blueprint and rebuild.

By removing structures that no longer serve us (old habits) and designing functional, beautiful spaces (new patterns), we create a home that reflects who we are and who we want to become.

Many are dissatisfied with their bodies, but how many truly pay attention to how their mind operates?

When the when illness takes over, we fall into a pattern of "once I've done X, then I can..." But anything that enters your awareness is worth addressing now. This way, when the time comes, you'll be the person who can rise to the occasion. I believe acceptance matters more than courage.

> *"The secret of change is to focus all your energy, not on fighting the old, but on building the new."*
> – Socrates.

The Echo of the Past: Replay and Its Impact on the Present.

We maybe unconsciously spend 95% of our time thinking about just 5% of our lives—the parts that feel broken. What's on your mental loop, playing over and over? Is it something harmonious, or does it bring discomfort?

Memories can become controlling forces. A painful childhood Christmas, for example, may cast a shadow over every holiday season. If we don't process our traumas, the body stores them, constantly reminding us of their weight. This creates a debt—carrying emotional interest that drains our present quality of life and stunts growth.

"When someone else designs you and then breaks your own measure of self-worth, it becomes almost impossible to open the gate and close the gap on your own."

Transformative elements

The Operating System: How We Shape Our Lives Through Inner Programming.

We all have an internal operating system guiding our thoughts, reactions, and behavior. This system is shaped by habits, perceptions, and how we respond to reality.

Real change requires examining this system, identifying what supports us and what holds us back.

By upgrading the system through conscious decisions, we can create a life of balance and alignment with our deepest intentions.

Within us is an unrelenting judge, attempting to control our thoughts and actions through constant criticism and expectations. Even with our intuition and awareness, we often fall into patterns of seeking justification or perfection.

When we allow these behaviors to shape us, we invite states of discomfort and imbalance.

. . .

What Holds You Back?

Often, we are our own greatest obstacles. Unconscious habits, perceptions, and thought patterns can block the path to well-being.

However, awareness gives us choice—the ability to change what doesn't serve us and embark on a journey of growth. *How Do We Hold Ourselves Back?*

1. *Unacceptable Perceptions*

When we fail to accept the good, we open the door to the bad. Like a hostile takeover, what we surrender control over invites its "friends" to occupy our lives.

- *Example:* Poor eating habits often come in groups—unhealthy foods trigger sugar cravings, low energy, and a desire for quick fixes.

Words and Their Opposites. "Every word invokes its opposite." – Goethe

- Every action has consequences; awareness of this can lead to clearer decisions.

2. *Denial as a Defense Mechanism*

Denial is often the last stronghold where we cling to hope, even if it's unsustainable. It prevents us from confronting reality and hinders change.

Input and Its Impact

If we lose control over what we allow into our lives—thoughts, emotions, or substances—the void fills itself.

As the saying goes: *"If you let in harmful input, it will invite its friends to visit."*

Healing and Shame

    1. *Salt in the Wound*

If someone throws salt at you, it only stings if you have an open wound.
This underscores the importance of healing your own wounds and establishing a healthy foundation.

    2. *Shame and Light*

Shame thrives in darkness. Awareness and honesty with yourself open the door to healing.

- When shame is illuminated, it loses its power.

People and Connections: "Understand people instead of leaving them."
We all seek resonance, often unconsciously. When we choose to understand people rather than reject them, we open doors to connections that can be healing for both us and others.

Systems That Hold Us Back

    1. *An Immature Inner Life*

When we fail to nurture the growth of our inner world, we risk becoming victims of our own inadequacies.

2. *Perception and Illusion*

What we see and hear appears real but is often shaped by the observer's perspective.

This can create a world of illusion, requiring constant defense because it isn't grounded in truth.

- *Question:* What illusions have I accepted as truth?

Working Through These Challenges

1. *Attention and Awareness*

Healing begins with attention. By focusing on what holds us back, we can transform it into strength.

2. *Taking Responsibility*

What in my behavior blocks health from entering my life? Answering this question honestly opens the door to change.

3. *Letting Go*

"You can't leave until you arrive." We must face what hinders us before moving forward.

What Helps You?

1. *Finding Nourishing Ground*

What you plant in matters. Choose environments, relationships, and habits that nourish, energize, and promote growth.

- What is your "nourishing ground"?

2. *Observation and Intention*

By examining what works and setting intentions for change, we can transform old patterns.
Our focus becomes a lever to create something new.

3. *New Experiences*

Each new experience offers fresh insight into your personality. They add to your self-knowledge and give you opportunities to evolve.

- "New personal experiences add new dimensions to your personality."

4. *Creating Ideal Conditions*

By designing environments that support positive change, you make it easier to grow.

What Harms You?

1. *Old Threads*

If we keep following the same patterns, we'll keep seeing the same signs on the "loop" we're driving. To break free, we must find an exit point.

- What old habits are holding you back?

2. *Unclear Goals and Direction*

Ambiguity and lack of clarity create stagnation. Ask yourself: "What chooses me? What do I want to choose for myself?"

3. *Pressure and Unrealistic Expectations*

Striving for perfection is impossible. We need to learn to let go and find balance.

- "It's hard to always be Superman. Flow is the way to go."

4. *Unconscious Behavior*

We're programmed to do what we know, even if it no longer serves us.

How Would You Redesign Your Operating System?

1. *Finding New Solutions*

- What do you want to eliminate from your system?
- What new elements do you want to incorporate?

2. *Long-Term Solutions*

Look for ways to change habits with lasting impact.
Choose solutions that support your future, not just short-term fixes.

3. *Avoiding Skewed Balance*

If you start from a place of imbalance, you risk undermining what's good. Align your internal compass.

4. *Taking Ownership of Your Experiences*

Your experiences set you apart, but they don't define you unless you let them.

Advice for Change

- Avoid ignorance: Ancient wisdom teaches that ignorance is the root of suffering. Knowledge and experience are your best defenses against illusion.

- Awareness and choice: Awareness gives us the power to choose growth. When we stop reacting unconsciously, we can choose new responses.

- Experience brings wisdom: What we live through and learn shapes us.
- *"Experience alone makes us wise and guards us against illusions."*

Ways to Strengthen Your Inner Operating System

- *Intention and Observation*

Meditation, conscious decision-making, and self-reflection break old patterns and create new pathways.

- *Knowledge and Self-Understanding*

Understanding your emotions, triggers, and strengths enhances your control over your reactions.

- *Developing New Habits*

Healthy habits support brain function and reduce the stress of constant self-regulation.

A Real-Life Story: Changing the System

Caleb found himself repeatedly in the same situations. He started projects with good intentions but quickly gave up, filled with doubt and impatience.

After examining his pattern, he realized his internal operating system was shaped by outdated habits and thoughts.

He began observing how he responded to challenges and implemented small steps to build willpower and confidence.

He wrote down his goals, meditated daily, and found ways to shift his mindset.

Over time, he experienced not only greater peace of mind but also improved ability to follow through on his aspirations.

Self-Reflecting Questions

1. What habits and thoughts in your operating system support you, and what needs to change?

2. How can you use conscious decision-making and observation to counteract old patterns?

3. What can you do today to strengthen your will and create a life aligned with your values and dreams?

Closing Words

Our operating system shapes how we experience life. By working with intention and awareness, we can transform old patterns and create a life based on balance and growth.

Every small step we take today strengthens our future and brings us closer to the quality of life we seek.

Answer the questions and meditate for 10 minutes. Reflect on what you are sensing after this work and write it down

Day 8

Communication – Bridges, Walls, and the Path to Health

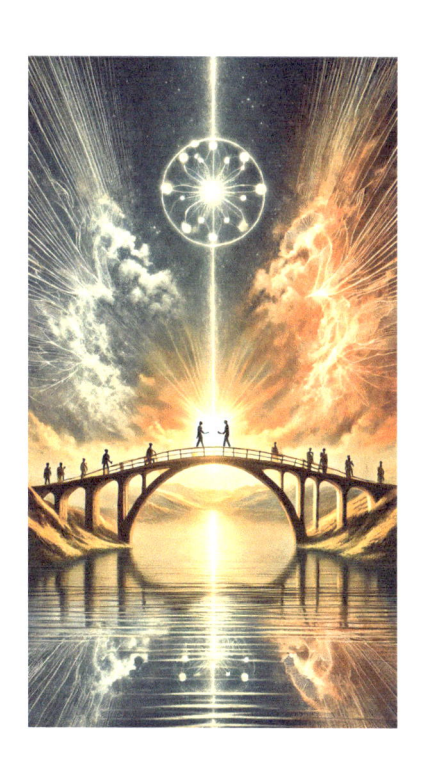

In this chapter we explore how mindful communication, built on respect, understanding, and self-awareness, fosters stronger connections, emotional growth, and inner peace, while guiding us to build bridges instead of walls in our relationships.

Take a deep breath and meditate for 5 minutes

The River and the Bridge

Communication is like a river flowing between two shores. It has the power to connect or divide, depending on how we build our bridges.

A strong, mindful bridge stands on pillars of respect, understanding, and self-awareness, allowing the river of dialogue to flow freely and nurture the connection.

However, when walls are built instead of bridges, the river becomes a barrier, cutting off connection and growth. By choosing to build bridges, we create pathways for healing, balance, and meaningful relationships.

"Nothing needs change as urgently as someone else's behavior."
– Oscar Wilde

Communication is like a landscape we navigate daily. Some paths are smooth and easy, while others are rocky and challenging. In every interaction, we make choices – do we build bridges that connect or walls that divide?

Through mindfulness, self-reflection, and intention, we can create relationships that heal, strengthen, and uplift.

. . .

Communication – Responsibility, Truth, and Inner Strength.

Communication can sometimes feel like a trade-off, where we excuse our behavior based on others.

To change how we connect with others, we must first change our thoughts and conversations.

It begins with taking responsibility for our role and words. Nothing genuine can be threatened, and no one can diminish you unless you allow it.

Transformative elements

The Foundation of Good Communication

To build strong relationships, we must listen with both heart and mind.

Listening requires maturity, sincerity, and a desire to understand. These qualities deepen emotional balance and connection.

We often perceive more than we understand, but in our unconscious state, we may turn off our sensors.

This tendency can lead to misunderstandings and disrespect, where we hear but do not connect. The biggest challenge in communication is when we listen not to understand but merely to reply.

Examples of Miscommunication:

- Repeating a story to different groups without considering the audience.
- Speaking loudly in a confined space and ignoring others' needs.
- Being preoccupied with your phone during a conversation.
- Taking without giving back – for example, attending a meal without helping out.

- Responding warmly to questions but failing to ask questions in return.

These situations illustrate communication gaps where we fail to connect or show respect for others.

Self-Centeredness and Its Effects

Self-centeredness, derived from the Greek root of the word *"idiot,"* is like a mud puddle no one wants to linger in. When everything revolves around us, we lose the nourishment connections provide. Relationships require balance, where giving and receiving coexist healthily.

"What you give is what you get."

Respect, much like nourishment, gives more than it takes. Practice uplifting others with your presence, and you'll foster deeper connections.

Path to Healthy Relationships

1. *Connect Instead of Correct:*

Most people struggle not with change itself but with how change is introduced to them.
Corrections diminish and can shut down connections.
Instead of correcting, focus on listening and relating.

2. *Acceptance*

Accepting others as they are, reflects how well we accept ourselves. Constantly trying to change others may indicate a lack of self-acceptance.

3. *Respect for Boundaries*

When we set boundaries with kindness and respect, we strengthen ourselves and our relationships. Those who respect our boundaries often grow closer to us.

Truth and Health
Health is living in alignment with truth. The words we use carry significant weight. Phrases like *"I can't"* are not just declarations; they become part of our reality.
Replacing them with *"I won't"* restores agency and taps into our inner power.
In toxic environments, some sew the pattern of *"I can't,"* creating a cycle of helplessness and learned powerlessness.

Breaking this pattern requires finding inner strength and using words consciously and powerfully.

> *Understanding Others and Ourselves:* "What are you going through right now that affects how you treat me?"

This question opens the door to deeper connection. It reminds us of the importance of seeing people as they are, rather than trying to change them.
Understanding begins when we accept both our strengths and weaknesses – as we can only accept others when we accept ourselves.

Corrections and Their Impact
Corrections, especially when delivered with disrespect, can diminish others. Instead of correcting, strive to understand.

- *"Most people struggle with how you try to change them, not the changes themselves."*

- Pay attention to what lies beneath – emotions often precede thoughts.

Nurturing Communication and Self-Awareness

Being a "nurturing soil" means creating a foundation where you respect your values and those of others.

Fostering trust and respect for others builds confidence and freedom within positive connections.

Communication Built on Understanding

1. *Listen Attentively*

Hearing others without preplanning your response enhances understanding.

Covey advised: *"Seek first to understand, then to be understood."*

2. *Understand Your Impact*

How do we express ourselves without dominating?
Recognizing when we're tempted to center communication on ourselves gives us the chance to improve.

3. *See Through Others' Perspectives*

People who often feel misunderstood rarely consider others' viewpoints.
Developing this skill enriches all relationships.

4. *Acknowledge Your Limitations*

Understanding what triggers insecurity or helplessness, is the first step in forming strong, healthy connections.

5. *Take Responsibility for Emotions*

We are accountable for our responses, whether they stem from fear, anger, or mistrust.

6. *Integrity in Communication*

To build trust, we must be open and honest, without placing undue burdens on others.

> "When you want to help others, tell them the truth. When you want to help yourself, tell them what they want to hear."
> – Thomas Sowell.

Healthy Communication – Key Elements
Healing communication relies on warmth, understanding, and shared safety. It creates fertile ground for growth and helps us release unhealthy patterns.

1. *Mindfulness:* Be present and listen without expectation or judgment.
2. *Connection:* Build bridges, not walls.
3. *Belonging:* Find security and worth in your relationships.

Strengthening Connections

1. *Listening:* Create space where others can speak freely without fear.

2. *Soft Boundaries:* Set limits with respect and warmth to avoid escalation.
3. *Solution-Focused Approach:* Agree on communication guidelines and solutions.

Connections and Their Role in Our Lives

We aim to form healthy connections that foster growth.

People who listen to us and make us feel valued create a nurturing environment.

Those who diminish us with negativity or neglect may need to be removed from our network – even if they are close family members.

Control and Relationships

Control often stems from a lack of control over one's own life.

Those who try to control others often lose touch with their inner selves. This leads to unconscious behaviors, such as being "remote-controlled" by others or allowing undue influence over one's life.

"Maturity is walking away from people and situations that threaten your peace of mind, self-respect, values, and self-worth."

Exercise: Who Controls You?

- Ask yourself: *"Who in my life is best at remote controlling me?"*
- Choose to step away from being a burden-bearer and become more independent.

Communication Without Awareness

Unconscious communication occurs when we fail to perceive

true needs and only interpret what we think we see. Combat this by staying aware and opening up to genuine emotions.

- *To conceal is to steal* – hiding your own needs or feelings blocks connection.
- *To share is to heal* – open communication creates space for connection and healing.

Confidence and Boundaries in Communication
If someone speaks to you disrespectfully:

- Step into your power.
- Say: *"It's not acceptable to talk to me that way."*

This boundary isn't just for them – it's also for you. Setting boundaries protects your balance and strengthens your self-respect.

A Real-Life Story

I met two sisters and asked them: *"What's the greatest stressor in your life?"* One replied without hesitation: *"The night shift."*
The other thought for a long time before answering: *"My brother."* The first sister added: *"I cut him out of my life ten years ago."*
So often, someone close to us is in deep imbalance.
Blood may be thicker than water, but the seeds life plants in our beginnings can cut deeply, leaving us powerless.

Self-Reflecting Questions

1. What habits might prevent you from connecting with those around you?

2. How can you show respect and love in your daily interactions?
3. What steps can you take to listen better and seek to understand rather than respond immediately?
4. Who in your inner circle provides you with the most warmth?

Final Words - Building Bridges

Communication is the foundation of healthy relationships and personal growth.

By prioritizing respect, understanding, and warmth, we can build bridges instead of walls.

Connecting rather than correcting is the key to creating a life filled with deeper relationships, peace, and balance.

Take responsibility for your words and actions. Use them with intention and power.

When you master your communication, you create space for growth, healing, and happiness.

Answer the questions and meditate for 10 minutes. Reflect on what you are sensing after this work and write it down.

Day 9

Energy – Where Do You Find It, and How Do You Use It?

This chapter explores the importance of managing and directing energy—spiritual, mental, emotional, and physical—to build balance, break cycles of fatigue, and create a fulfilling life by focusing on what nourishes rather than depletes.

Take a deep breath and meditate for 5 minutes

The Reservoir and the Streams

Energy is like a reservoir that feeds streams flowing into different areas of your life—spiritual, mental, emotional, and physical.

If the reservoir is full, the streams flow freely, nourishing everything they touch. But when the reservoir runs low due to neglect, overuse, or poor management, the streams dry up, leaving parts of your life barren.

By intentionally replenishing the reservoir—through rest, mindful habits, and healthy choices—you ensure that each stream flows steadily, creating a balanced and fulfilling life.

In day 4, "The health box"—I learned about a balanced environment that nourishes both my body and mind. By cultivating intentional habits, practicing self-respect, and removing distractions, I enable myself to grow and embrace simplicity.

Energy is the essence of life—it drives us forward and helps us tackle life's challenges. The key isn't just how much energy we have, but how we use it.

By managing our energy wisely, we can enhance balance, well-being, and overall quality of life.

Have you ever noticed how contagious energy can be? For instance, when someone yawns near you, it's hard not to follow suit. The same applies to emotional energy—it spreads. That's why it's essential to choose environments and people that nourish your energy rather than drain it.

> *"Don't tell anyone what you are doing until it's done. Outside energy can throw off goals. That's law."*
> —Wisdom Words

Attention and Energy
What you give attention to receives your energy.

> As Henry Ford put it: *"Most people spend more time and energy avoiding problems than trying to solve them."*

When we focus on the right things, we boost our ability to overcome challenges. Freedom comes from having nothing to hide and using energy where it has the greatest value. Where do you find the energy to persevere when the going gets tough?

True freedom is found in transparency and deliberate use of energy to build physical, mental, and emotional strength.

The Man Who Couldn't Get Off the Couch
Once, there was a man who spent his days working tirelessly to build and create. After long hours, he would come home, exhausted, and collapse on the couch. He'd start thinking about all the things he still needed to do and how he would do them. His mind became flooded with tasks and details.

. . .

The more he thought, the heavier the burden grew, until he couldn't bring himself to move from the couch.

Deep down, he felt proud of himself for constantly thinking about his responsibilities. Yet, he remained stuck, unable to act.

The Lesson – Mental Fatigue is Real

Our brain consumes the most energy of any organ in our body. The more we dwell on what we need to do, *without acting*, the more drained we feel. Energy is spent on overthinking rather than solving problems.

Transformative elements

Breaking the Cycle

- *Start with small actions.* Taking the first step shifts the burden from the brain and lightens the load.
- *Reduce worry with action.* Focus less on how, and more on just starting.

Action frees the mind. By moving and taking those initial steps, the fatigue begins to lift, and fresh energy emerges.

The Energy Pyramid

The Energy Pyramid explains how different types of energy interact and influence our well-being. Each layer is critical for building balance and achieving success in life.

Spiritual Energy – The Inner Foundation

Spiritual energy comes from believing in yourself, having a purpose, and connecting to what truly matters in life. It helps you face adversity and stay focused on long-term goals.

1. *Mental Energy – Mastering Focus*

Mental energy determines how effectively you use your mind. It fuels creativity, problem-solving, and concentration.

- Scattered mental energy makes it hard to focus. Practices like meditation can help you direct it purposefully.

2. *Emotional Energy – The Quality of Connections*

Emotional energy governs how we relate to ourselves and others. It influences the quality of both inner dialogue and external relationships.

- Balanced emotional energy leads to clearer, more positive, and constructive communication.

3. *Physical Energy – The Tank's Capacity*

Physical energy is the foundation of how much energy you have each day. It's fueled by movement, sleep, and nutrition.

- It's the "fuel" that powers everything else. Without it, engaging spiritual, mental, or emotional energy becomes difficult.

Why Does This Matter?
Building and maintaining the Energy Pyramid is the key to holistic well-being. When all layers support one another, you can reach your highest energy and growth potential.

―――

A Real-Life Story

A man caught in a cycle of exhaustion realized that his thoughts were draining him. He decided to change his approach.

1. He nourished his body with wholesome food, regaining physical energy.
2. He went for a walk, finding mental clarity and peace.
3. He wrote down simple goals for the next day, reducing the overwhelm.

Gradually, he felt more energized, balanced, and clear in his daily life. He learned that both physical and mental energy rely on proper management and rest.

Self-Reflecting Questions

1. What aspect of your Energy Pyramid needs attention?
2. What gives you the most energy, and what drains it?

Relaxation or Shutdown?

- Are you watching, eating, or scrolling to relax, or are you simply shutting down?
- Happiness arises when you make multiple right choices *simultaneously focusing* on what brings balance and fulfilment.

Life in Motion - The world is always in motion

- Waves dance with the wind.
- Grass grows effortlessly.
- Fish swim freely.

Finding your body's natural rhythm—like taking a simple walk—can reawaken both your body and mind. The universe sends you signals—trust your intuition, it won't lead you astray.

Practical Tips for Energy Management

1. *Track your energy:* Write down what drains and what energizes you. Reduce what depletes you and increase what nourishes you.

2. *Design your day:*
   - Start mornings with meditation, exercise, or a nutritious breakfast.
   - Choose activities that bring joy and strength.

3. *Fuel for body and mind:*
   - Foods like green tea boost focus and strengthen memory.

More Self-Reflecting Questions

1. Where is my energy going today—am I nourishing or depleting it?

2. What can I do today to improve my energy levels?

3. What habits can I adopt to have a positive long-term impact on my energy?

Closing Words - Choosing What Nourishes You

What matters most isn't the amount of energy you have but how you use it. A clear purpose and deliberate choices unlock energy and create freedom.

By shifting from what drains you to what nourishes you, life becomes more powerful and balanced. *"Where attention goes, energy flows."*

Answer the questions and meditate for 10 minutes. Reflect on what you are sensing after this work and write it down

Day 10

The Brain – The Power Station That Governs Our Lives

T his chapter emphasizes the importance of nurturing the brain through balanced routines, nutrition, rest, and exercise to enhance focus, clarity, and overall well-being, while demonstrating how small, intentional actions can lead to transformative mental and physical health.

Taka a deep breath and meditate for 5 minutes

The Brain as the Lighthouse

The brain is like a lighthouse, guiding the ship of your life through calm seas and storms alike. Its light represents focus, clarity, and direction, but to keep it shining brightly, the power station within must be well-maintained.

Fuel it with balanced routines, nutritious food, restful sleep, and exercise, and the light beams strong and steady, illuminating your path. Neglect it, and the light flickers, leaving you vulnerable to the chaos of distraction and fatigue.

In day 5, "The mind"- I focus on mastering my thoughts by breaking old patterns, practicing mindfulness, and developing new mental habits that help me stay present, find balance, and support my personal growth.

The brain is the most energy-intensive organ in the body, managing every aspect of our lives. Taking care of it is crucial for well-being, focus, and success.

A solid routine is more impactful than perfect plans—what we do daily shapes our lives and future.

The prefrontal cortex, responsible for organization and decision-making, performs best in the early part of the day. But how can we maintain its effectiveness as the day progresses?

Distraction: The Brain's Biggest Enemy
Distractions are one of the greatest challenges of modern life. They destroy focus, increase stress, and consume a lot of mental energy.

By slowing down brain waves and establishing clear habits, we can reduce the brain's load and improve overall well-being. Caring for the brain requires a balance of nutrition, rest, and routine.

My Story - Cold-Water Swimming, the Greatest Gift in My Life

In 2009, I started cold-water swimming, and it has been the greatest gift life has given me.

As someone who has struggled with depression since childhood, nothing has been as helpful. I always leave the water singing—it feels like dressing in nature itself.

When you swim in the ocean, you're not just enjoying nature; you're immersing yourself in it.

Transformative elements

Tools to Strengthen the Brain

1. *Review and Compass Adjustment*
   - Take time weekly to evaluate what's working well and what needs to change.
   - Write down goals and prioritize them.
   - Talk to someone you trust to gain new ideas and perspectives.
2. *Brain Nutrition*

- Healthy fats, like avocado oil, hemp oil, or flaxseed oil, support healthy brain function.
- Take one tablespoon daily for every 25 kg of body weight.
- This nutrition reduces cravings for sweets and promotes mental balance and energy.
3. *Rest and Relaxation*
    - Meditation provides the brain with essential rest and renewal. It reduces stress and increases clarity.
    - Regular, high-quality sleep is vital for brain health.
4. *Exercise*
    - Regular physical activity strengthens the body and mind, lowers blood pressure, and improves mood.
    - It increases blood flow and oxygen to the brain, enhancing focus and mental well-being.

Exercise: The Key to Clarity and Calm

I firmly believe that one of the best things we can do for our brains is to exercise. When faced with an overwhelming task, I start by moving—whether it's a walk, a run, or a workout.

The effects are remarkable. After exercising, the task no longer feels as daunting.

The associated stress diminishes for me by as much as 77%, and the most anxiety-provoking aspects fade away.

Clarity replaces the fog, and I feel energized and focused enough to tackle what once seemed impossible.

Exercise acts as a reset button for the mind, clearing unnecessary worries and opening pathways for solutions. It's my way of inviting both the brain and body to work together for well-being and success.

. . .

The Benefits of Exercise for Body and Mind:

- *Lowers Blood Pressure:* Regular exercise supports healthy blood pressure and circulation.
- *Stronger Heart:* The heart chambers expand and strengthen, improving cardiac function and endurance.
- *Increased Capillary Density in Muscles:* More capillaries deliver oxygen and nutrients to worked muscles.
- *Stronger Skeletal Muscles:* Improved balance and posture result from stronger muscles.
- *Stronger Bones and Tendons:* Regular activity reduces the risk of fractures and tendon injuries.
- *Improved Blood Lipid Balance:* Decreases LDL (bad cholesterol) and increases HDL (good cholesterol), promoting cardiovascular health.
- *Elevated Mood and Joy:* Releases endorphins that boost mood and reduce stress.
- *Enhanced Brain Function:* Improves blood flow to the brain, supporting better concentration and memory.
- *Increased Oxygen Uptake:* A more efficient respiratory system improves overall endurance and energy.
- *Better Sleep:* Regular exercise fosters deeper, more restorative sleep.
- *Increased Muscle Mass:* Reduces age-related muscle loss and maintains strength.
- *Strength Gains in the First 8 Weeks:* Strength can increase by 40–60% in the first eight weeks.
- *Weight Management:* Body fat can decrease by 3–4% over 10 weeks, improving overall health.

My Work as a Personal Trainer and the Impact of Cold-Water Swimming.

As a personal trainer for 22 years, I've prioritized creating sessions that foster both physical and mental well-being. A particular focus has been on providing brain rest for my clients. The brain, being the body's most energy-demanding organ, benefits greatly from moments of mindful connection to the present.

In my sessions, I use a stopwatch to structure the workout into circuits with three exercises and three rounds. When the timer beeps, clients move to the next exercise.

This flow reduces mental clutter and enhances focus. I encourage them to direct their attention inward, focusing on the body part being worked on to increase awareness and deepen the exercise.

To build discipline, I emphasize adding five extra repetitions at the end of a set. This sends a message from the mind to the body: *"I'm in charge, not you."*

This discipline spills over into other areas of life, positively affecting work, relationships, and personal goals.

I've had the honor of accompanying over 100 people on their first ocean swim. Everyone except one immediately said: *"When are we going again?"*

People are surprised by how manageable it is compared to their expectations. Cold-water swimming has a transformative power—victories achieved in the water carry over to other areas of life.

A Lesson in Changing the Game

A man dreamed of becoming an NFL coach in the U.S.

His unique approach was to teach players to stop over-thinking and instead rely on intuition and trained responses. His method aimed to minimize cognitive effort during games, allowing players to direct all their energy toward action rather than decision-making.

Though his approach was innovative, his first four interviews with teams were unsuccessful—his methods were considered too unconventional. But he persisted.

In his fifth interview, he convinced the team's management and got the job. That year, the team won the NFL championship, one of the highest achievements in American football.

Key Takeaways

Sometimes, the unfamiliar and unconventional lead to the greatest success. Trusting the process, rather than clinging to old habits, can transform outcomes.

A Real-Life Story: Turning Over a New Leaf

Kefas, a thirty-something engineer, experienced constant stress and fatigue that affected his performance at work and his relationships with his family. Feeling dissatisfied, he decided to make small but deliberate changes to his daily life.

He took action:

- *Weekly Evaluation:* Kefas set aside time every Sunday to review what he was doing well and what he could improve.
- *Improving His Diet:* By adding healthy fats, like avocado oil, to his breakfast, he noticed more stable energy levels and reduced cravings for sweets.
- *Daily Meditation:* With 10 minutes of evening meditation, he achieved greater calm and focus.
- *Increasing Physical Activity:* Kefas began taking walks three times a week, which improved his mood and boosted his physical energy.

After a few weeks, Kefas noticed a significant change—he had more energy, clearer focus, and stronger control over his life. These small adjustments had a compounding effect on his overall well-being.

Self-Reflecting Questions

1. What do I need to let go of to make space for something new in my life?
2. Who in my environment provides the support and peace I need on this journey?
3. How can I balance challenges and skills to nurture my inner drive?

Closing Words

The brain governs our lives, but we can influence how it operates by caring for it.

Good habits, nutrition, and regular exercise help the brain grow and function better. By incorporating these elements into daily life, we lay the foundation for a brighter future—not only for ourselves but for those who are around us.

Answer the questions and meditate for 10 minutes. Reflect on what you are sensing after this work and write it down

Day 11

The Journey – Growing, Learning and Evolving

In this chapter we look at life as a journey of growth, learning, and evolution with each step we take. This journey demands courage, resilience, and inner peace to let go of what holds us back and embrace new opportunities. When we focus on creating something fresh and fulfilling instead of remaining trapped in old patterns, our lives bloom and thrive.

Taka a deep breath and meditate for 5 minutes

Metaphor for The Journey – Growing, Learning, and Evolving
"Life is a winding river, flowing toward the ocean of self-discovery. Along the way, it carves through stone, nourishes the soil, and creates its path. Like the river, your journey demands patience and resilience, as each twist and turn shapes your inner landscape, bringing you closer to your true self."

In day 6, "Building a New personality", I delve into how becoming more self-aware, confronting my inner struggles, and embracing new experiences can help me transform old patterns, cultivate inner prosperity, and bring harmony to both my mind and body.

"Men rush ahead further when they have no idea where they are going."
– Voltaire

My Story

As a young boy, I was placed in situations I didn't want to be in. What did that change in me?

This created a "model" – an automatic system I unknowingly followed as an adult, recreating similar scenarios even when I had the choice to do otherwise.

Transformative elements

Key Aspects of the Journey

1. *Creating New Experiences*

By gradually making the right decisions, we build the courage to release what no longer serves us.

Repetition and persistence open doors to new possibilities and strengthen our inner drive.

2. *Choosing the Right Companions*

The people around us significantly influence our growth.

Those who provide peace and security become invaluable allies on life's path.

3. *Celebrating Yourself*

The greatest gift you can receive is yourself. By nurturing self-awareness and self-respect, you'll find peace and balance.

> "The good life is a process, not a state of being. It is a direction, not a destination."
> – Carl Rogers

The Path to Growth and Change

1. *Mental Preparation*

Everything in life is preparation. Each step you take, every challenge you overcome, prepares you for the next chapter in life.

- "We strive to find the place where preparation meets opportunity."

2. *The Courage to Let Go*

Letting go of what hinders us creates space for new experiences.
Life rewards courage with opportunities that lead to growth and well-being.

- "If you have the courage to say goodbye to what no longer serves you, life will open doors to new possibilities."

3. *Taking Risks*

Allowing fear to hold you back is worse than failing.
Mistakes are part of growth, and taking the first step reveals the path ahead.

"More is lost by indecision than by wrong decision." – Cicero

The Key to Happiness
Happiness lies in making many right decisions at once and repeating them daily.
Over time, repetition becomes a stronger force than singular experiences.

- "Training, not trying."

The Journey of Inner Change – Removing the Impact of Circumstances.

It's easy to remove someone from harmful circumstances, but removing the impact of those circumstances from the individual requires much more effort.

This process demands deep introspection, acknowledgment of the root cause, and a willingness to change.

Our lives are shaped by experiences, but how we process them determines our growth and well-being.

What Holds You Back?

What patterns or attitudes within you prevent you from opening the door to health and happiness?

These patterns often act as invisible operating systems unconsciously adopted from past experiences.

Understanding Triggers – What Drives the Root Causes?

Life isn't just a problem to solve but a reality to experience. Success begins with identifying the root cause of the problem.

A tree has roots that determine its fruits. What fruits do you want in your life? What do those roots look like?

Recognizing the roots that produce the outcomes we experience – whether joy, fear, hope, or guilt – allows us to change them through intention and observation.

Repetition is Stronger Than Experience

Repetition shapes behavior. When we are stuck in patterns that don't serve us, we are prone to seek fleeting pleasures to numb the lack of meaning.

"When you cannot find a deep sense of meaning, you distract yourself with pleasure."
– Viktor Frankl

Overcoming Resistance
Resistance often lies in the things we fear facing.

As Carl Jung said: *"People will do anything, no matter how absurd, to avoid facing their own souls."*

To achieve change, we must:

1. Identify the Trigger: What causes the resistance?
2. Apply Awareness and Intention: Build self-awareness and take deliberate steps.
3. Balance Challenge and Ability: Don't demand too much of yourself but push for growth.

Breaking Free from Ruts – The Journey of Inner Transformation
When we take our foot off the gas pedal, balance emerges. Stress decreases, and we find ourselves "unstuck," able to move forward.

Life is a common journey that follows a pattern: we get stuck, lose direction, and then – breakthrough. This pattern reflects our work, personal lives, and approach to challenges.

The Hole We Are Trapped In
To break free from a rut, we must recognize the hole we're stuck in. It could be a fear of change, unresolved pain, or clinging to false beliefs. Freud described the unconscious as an "iceberg" – we only see the tip, while the bulk of the issue lies beneath the surface.

. . .

Change and Resistance

Change causes disruption, and our brains are programmed to resist anything that threatens the status quo. However, understanding that this disruption is necessary for growth opens new opportunities.

We have a strong tendency to get stuck in the fear of change, missing the window of opportunity in the present moment.

Life Reflections

1. Experience is like a toothpick: It's meant for personal use. What worked for one person may not work for you.
2. People build walls where they should build bridges: Isolation often replaces connection.
3. Life's trials: Life brings us back to the starting point when we fail to learn from experiences.
4. Fear of others' opinions: This is life's greatest trap, often hindering progress.
5. When the student is ready, the teacher appears: Knowledge arises when we are prepared to receive it.
6. Life moves on: Whether you worry or not, life continues its course.
7. Satisfied needs don't help: Being too content with the current state stunts growth.

Practical Steps to Break Free

1. Identify the Resistance: Ask yourself, "What's holding me back?"
2. Observation and Intention: Recognize patterns holding you back and set deliberate goals.
3. Let Go of False Beliefs: Allow new ideas to shape you and release old ones.

4. Be Open to Change: Though uncomfortable, change is necessary for growth.
5. Build Bridges, Not Walls: Seek connections instead of isolating yourself.

Inspirational Quotes

"The one who ensures others' success has already ensured their own." – Confucius

"Life is not a problem to be solved, but a reality to be experienced." – Søren Kierkegaard

"People will do anything, no matter how absurd, to avoid facing their own souls." – Carl Jung

A Real-Life Story: The Destination Is the Journey Itself

Claudia had long been stuck in the same patterns. She regretted missed opportunities and felt dissatisfied with her life.

One day, she decided to take small steps – writing down what she was grateful for and setting goals.

Over time, she became aware of where she needed to let go and who brought her peace and encouragement.

She began making small, deliberate decisions daily and found herself thriving. Claudia realized that the journey was not the destination but how she approached it.

By consciously choosing each step, she created a new life where growth and well-being were at the forefront.

Self-Reflecting Questions

1. What do I need to let go of to make space for something new in my life?

2. Who in my environment provides the support and peace I need on this journey?

3. How can I balance challenges and skills to nurture my inner drive?

Answer the questions and meditate for 10 minutes. Reflect on what you are sensing after this work and write it down

Day 12

Are you a Prisoner?

In this chapter we explore the journey from self-imposed emotional imprisonment, rooted in past traumas and fear of others' opinions, to freedom achieved through self-acceptance, forgiveness, and living in alignment with one's own values.

Take a deep breath and meditate for 5 minutes

The Key to the Self-Made Prison

Emotional imprisonment is like being locked in a cell you've built yourself. The walls are made of fear, shame, and the weight of others' opinions.

The key to freedom has always been within your reach, but it requires courage to pick it up and unlock the door.

Forgiveness, self-acceptance, and living by your values are the steps that lead you out. As you walk free, you realize the cell was never locked—it was the belief in your own limitations that held you captive.

In day 7, "The 5% syndrome" I dove into the concept of my internal "operating system," uncovering how outdated habits and recurring thought patterns consume 95% of my mental energy. By taking actionable steps, I learn to redesign this system, creating a more conscious, balanced, and fulfilling life.

What are your initial reactions? When you present your case to your people, do you carry shame? Discomfort in the body, often lingering from past traumas, signals unresolved issues. Although it may lessen over time, its presence remains.

We often create mental narratives—scenarios where others wrong us, we expose them, and exact revenge. Upon reflection, we realize: this stems from our own shame seeking release. Every thought, every reaction, mirrors what resides within us.

The reactions of others often reveal more about them than about us. Recognizing this brings freedom and peace.

Reading stories about resilient characters who stand firm in their truth despite challenges can be deeply healing.

My Story - Vulnerability and Growth

My environment was not equipped to meet my needs. *"I internalized the rules: don't speak, don't trust, don't believe."* No one listened; there were no lifelines to grasp, no healthy figure I could rely on.

At a young age, I was sent to the countryside, drowning in a growing sense of rejection.

At six years old, after spending 30 days away, I eagerly anticipated my father's arrival to pick me up. He called and asked if I would like to stay another month, and I said yes. I felt like nothing, owning nothing. I decided to get back at him.

I asked my sister, *"Is it better to skip putting toothpaste on the brush or to put toothpaste on my finger and skip the brush?"* At six years old, I had already become my own punisher.

Childhood Rejection and Self-Blame

Rejection from a parent at a young age can feel overwhelming.

Being six and experiencing unmet desires and needs can instill a lasting sense of being *"nothing, owning nothing."*

The story of the toothbrush and toothpaste is a poignant illustration of how children take on guilt and responsibility that isn't theirs.

Becoming one's own punisher at such a young age is a stark

reminder of how early patterns of self-blame and punishment emerge for situations beyond our control.

The Path to Healing:

1. *Acknowledging the Pain*

Facing these memories is a significant step. You are no longer the six-year-old who experienced this, but the emotions deserve to surface and be validated.

2. *Forgiveness – for Yourself and Others*

Forgiveness isn't about excusing behavior or denying feelings; it's about freeing yourself from the weight of the past. It liberates you from burdens carried too long.

3. *Rebuilding Trust*

Challenge the belief that you cannot speak, trust, or believe. Find safe people or communities to rely on and begin crafting new patterns with them.

4. *Releasing Self-Blame*

Remember, you were a child who needed love, support, and a listening ear. You did what you could to survive and remain whole in a difficult situation. There is no shame in needing protection.

5. *Redefining Yourself*

You are more than your past. Begin rediscovering who you are without these patterns.

. . .

The Opinions of Others

One of humanity's greatest traps is the fear of others' opinions. Seeing yourself through someone else's eyes is dangerous.

- It's impossible to truly know what others think.
- Opinions are fluid, influenced by their personal state of mind.
- Letting others define you borders on losing control of your own identity.

Caring too much about pleasing others can diminish your authentic self. True words and thoughts are living forces that define who you are.

Real-Life Story: Letting Go of the Fear of Others' Opinions

Peter always felt the need to please others. Meticulous at work, he earned a good reputation but still felt empty. He constantly thought, *"What will they think if I do this?"*

One day, Peter asked himself, *"Why does it matter what they think?"* He made a list of his own values and strengths and decided to follow them regardless of others' opinions.

As he began standing firm in his truth, he started making decisions that reflected his needs and desires. Though he faced criticism, he found freedom and relief in trusting his own judgment.

Thoughts on Vulnerability and Strength

Vulnerability is often mistaken for weakness, but it is one of our greatest strengths.

As Ernest Hemingway wrote:

> "The best people possess a feeling for beauty, the courage to take risks, the discipline to tell the truth, the capacity for sacrifice. Ironically, their virtues make them vulnerable; they are often wounded, sometimes destroyed."

Vulnerability makes us human and connects us to others. Though it sometimes leads to pain, every experience fosters growth and depth.

Self-reflecting Questions

1. How does fear of others' opinions impact your decisions and sense of self?
2. What steps can you take today to trust your judgment and let go of the need for approval?
3. How can you respond to shame or discomfort in a healthy way, using it as an opportunity for growth?

Final Words

> "I learned long ago never to wrestle with a pig. You get dirty, and besides, the pig likes it."
> – George Bernard Shaw

Fear and self-centeredness grow in the soil of unhealthy thoughts and circumstances.

They lead to harmful actions—toward both ourselves and others.

When fear governs us, we begin to believe that no one else can meet our needs.

We resort to our own measures, often at the expense of self-respect and trust.

Answer the questions and meditate for 10 minutes. Reflect on what you are sensing after this work and write it down

Day 13
Embracing What Is – You Don't Know What You've Got Until It's Gone

This Chapter explores the importance of appreciating the present, letting go of past patterns, and fostering love and respect in relationships as the keys to inner peace and true happiness.

Take a deep breath and meditate for 5 minutes

The Garden in Bloom

Life is like a garden, full of flowers, trees, and fruits that thrive when nurtured with care and attention. But often, we focus on what's missing—a flower that hasn't bloomed or a tree that bears no fruit—forgetting to appreciate the vibrant beauty already before us.

When the seasons change and the garden fades, we realize too late the richness it held. By tending to the garden as it is, watering its roots with love and respect, we cultivate not only growth but gratitude for its present abundance.

In day 8, "Communication", I explored how practicing mindful communication—grounded in respect, understanding, and self-awareness—helps me foster stronger connections, support emotional growth, and cultivate inner peace.

By focusing on building bridges instead of walls, I nurture healthier and more meaningful relationships.

My Story

One evening, after a long day, my wife came home. The day before, she had unfairly taken out her stress on me, and I had been hurt by it. She was clearly exhausted and not in a balanced state.

Instead of meeting her with irritation, I smiled, hugged her, and said, "Welcome home."

The next day, she told me, "You let me be myself without judging me." That small moment changed everything.

It taught me that little gestures in our interactions can transform our relationships.

The Energy We Give

Everything is energy. What we put out into the world is what we receive in return. Those who constantly seek to take will never feel truly fulfilled.

By nurturing others—especially when they seem least deserving—we create genuine connection and purpose.

The Subconscious: Hidden Influences from the Past

Our subconscious shapes our behavior without our awareness. It stores past experiences, patterns, and emotions that silently guide us. Only when we become aware of these patterns can we choose to change them.

My Story: A Journey Toward Self-Awareness and Freedom

As a young boy, I was sent to the countryside—a place I never wanted to go. I was placed with people who couldn't provide the care I needed, while my family was too preoccupied to notice my struggles. I felt unwanted and unworthy.

This experience stayed with me, unknowingly shaping my life.

As an adult, I repeatedly found myself in places I didn't want to be, both physically and emotionally. Like my time in the countryside, I felt trapped with no way out.

I realized that my patterns were rooted in childhood: being in the wrong places with the wrong people, accepting unhealthy circumstances.

The Inner Journey

As an adult, I saw that my patterns weren't just shaped by my circumstances but also by how I had responded to them. Though no one was telling me what to do anymore, I still followed the same script.

I lived by unspoken rules I had unknowingly created in childhood—rules about staying silent, accepting what was, and not believing in change.

These rules were no longer helpful; they were like an old radio program playing in the background, even though no one was listening.

Finding Freedom

Acknowledging this wasn't easy, but it was the first step toward change. I realized I was no longer bound by my past unless I allowed myself to be.

Letting go of old beliefs and patterns required courage, but it also gave me the freedom to choose a new path.

Today, I know I have the power to decide where I want to be, what I want to do, and with whom.

I've learned that the self-confidence and self-worth I build are the keys to breaking free from old chains.

The Lesson

When we let go of the past, take responsibility for our lives, and create new patterns, we can finally live in the present—free from the places we never wanted to be.

Transformative elements

Acknowledging the Present

Many of us wish we could turn back time and appreciate what we had. I'll be the first to raise my hand and admit it.

As a personal trainer for 22 years, I've noticed that those who achieve the best results are often people who have recently gone through a breakup. *Why is that?*

Perhaps it's because we often fail to appreciate what we have and instead focus on chasing something new—something we think will bring us happiness but often doesn't.

When we are stuck in the wrong role or place in life, we tend to believe that others have it better.

We focus on what is missing in our lives instead of valuing what we already have.

As Ecclesiastes reminds us:

"*I undertook great projects: I built houses, planted vineyards, gathered silver and gold... But when I surveyed all that my hands had done, it was all meaningless, a chasing after the wind.*"

This passage reminds us that external achievements can never fill internal emptiness.

Seeking Happiness in the Wrong Places: We often live with the illusion that happiness awaits us at the next destination.

- "When I get in shape, everything will be better."
- "When I have enough money, I'll be happy."
- "When my partner changes, our relationship will be perfect."

Yet when we achieve these goals, the emptiness often remains. This is because inner dissatisfaction follows us, regardless of external circumstances. True happiness doesn't come from the outside; it is created within.

Respect and Love: The Foundations of Relationships

Men crave respect; women crave love. When these fundamental needs are met, relationships flourish. Achieving this balance requires awareness and effort.

- *Men:* When they feel respected, they grow stronger in their roles.
- *Women:* When they feel loved and secure, they find the strength to give more of themselves.

Shame: How It Keeps Us Stuck

Shame can hold us captive unless we learn to work through it. It manifests in many ways.

1. *A False Self:* We build our identity on mistakes or others' judgments.
2. *Unmet Expectations:* When our dreams don't materialize, we feel powerless.
3. *Compassion and Identity:* By meeting shame with compassion, we can gradually release it and build a stronger sense of self.

Embracing What Is

Learning to value life as it is—rather than always seeking more—leads to inner peace.

This isn't easy; it requires mindfulness and practice.

When we nurture relationships with love and respect, they flourish, bringing purpose and joy into our lives.

Self-Reflecting Questions

1. What in your life can you begin to appreciate today?

2. How can you give more of yourself in your relationships?

3. What steps can you take to break old patterns and build a new foundation?

Final Words

Embracing what is, is the path to true happiness. By looking inward, working through the past, and offering love and respect, we discover life's true value.

This journey leads to freedom and peace—not only for ourselves but also for those around us.

Answer the questions and meditate for 10 minutes. Reflect on what you are sensing after this work and write it down

Day 14
Habits and Lifestyle Development The Path to Balance and Well-Being

This chapter explores the role of habits in shaping our lives, offering practical strategies for creating supportive routines, building self-awareness, and introducing positive habits through small, consistent steps to achieve lasting balance and personal growth.

Take a deep breath and meditate for 5 minutes

The Bricklayer's Journey
Building a balanced life is like constructing a sturdy house brick by brick. Each habit you form is a brick laid carefully, with purpose and precision.

The foundation is self-awareness, and the mortar is consistency—the glue that holds everything together. Some bricks take time to place, and mistakes may happen, but each one contributes to the strength and stability of your house.

Over time, these small, deliberate actions create a solid structure—a life built on balance, resilience, and well-being.

In day 4, "Health Box", I learned a balanced environment that nourishes both my body and mind.

By cultivating intentional habits, practicing self-respect, and removing distractions, I enable myself to grow and embrace simplicity.

In day 9, "The Energy", I delved into the importance of managing and directing my energy—spiritual, mental, emotional, and physical.

. . .

By focusing on what nourishes me rather than what depletes me, I work to build balance, break cycles of fatigue, and create a fulfilling life.

Integrity and a Supportive Environment

> *"The chains of habit are generally too light to be felt until they are too strong to be broken."*
> – Samuel Johnson

Habits bind us in chains, and our needs tie us down.

We are often stuck in a cycle where habits control us: rigid schedules, constant busyness, and demanding decisions push us toward short-term fixes—quick carbs, extra caffeine, or alcohol.

We flee from our physical and mental needs, allowing habits to trap us in reactive patterns, where the mind dissolves into self-neglect and the body cries out for new stimulations.

Transformative elements

Steps Toward Greater Awareness

1. How aware are you of your daily habits and their long-term effects on your future?
2. How can you cultivate new habits that promote growth and strength instead of short-term solutions?
3. What would you do today if you chose what is best for your body and mind with the future in mind?

Breaking the cycle requires re-evaluating the habits shaping your days. Growth in self-awareness involves reclaiming control by seeking healthy solutions from within.

Walking again with increased awareness, moving slower, and respecting your needs paves the way for balance and fulfillment.

Sneaking in Good Habits – Through the Back Door of Consciousness

Improving quality of life begins with small, consistent changes that we subtly weave into daily life. By investing in a better tomorrow and reducing unnecessary stressors, we can create balance and well-being that enhance both short- and long-term happiness.

Daily Habits to Enhance Awareness and Well-Being

1. *Start Your Day Calmly*
    - Finish your morning shower with cold water to awaken your body.
    - Write "morning pages" to clear your mind and gain clarity.
    - Meditate for a few minutes to set a positive mental tone.

2. *Move Daily*
    - Choose movement you enjoy, whether it's dancing, walking, or running.
    - Exercise helps reduce tension and release stress.

3. *Plan Meaningful Experiences*
    - Organize your day with activities and people that energize and bring you joy.

4. *Supportive Nutrition and Supplements*
    - *Ginkgo biloba:* Enhances blood flow and cognitive function.
    - *Acidophilus:* Supports digestion and well-being.
    - *Creatine and Glutamine*: Aid in physical recovery.

- *Vitamin D and Magnesium:* Promote sleep and strengthen the body.
- *Chamomile Tea in the Evening:* Encourages relaxation and prepares for sleep.

5. *Evening Routine for Better Sleep*
   - Avoid blue light (e.g., screens) before bed.
   - Play board games or dance to connect with family or friends.

The Habit Formation Process – Four Key Elements

1. *Cue:* The trigger that signals your brain to initiate the habit, often unconsciously.
2. *Craving:* The motivation that drives the habit—you don't crave junk food itself but the feeling it provides.
3. *Response:* The execution of the habit. If it's too challenging, it may hinder follow-through.
4. *Reward:* The feeling you get after completing the habit—or the lack thereof, which can lead to dissatisfaction.

Building Positive Habits

1. *Make It Obvious:* Ensure the cue is visible. Remove unwanted triggers.
2. *Make It Attractive:* Find ways to make the new habit appealing and eliminate those that don't serve you.
3. *Make It Easy:* Start with simple habits and make undesirable habits more complex.
4. *Make the Reward Clear:* Celebrate your progress toward your goals.

Creating "Master-Level Habits". Habits that promote physical, mental, and social well-being:

1. *Quality Sleep* – The foundation of balance.
2. *Enjoyable Movement* – Activities that bring joy and energy.
3. *Engaging Hobbies* – Nourish the mind and spark creativity.
4. *Meditation* – Provides calm and clarity.
5. *Healthy Social Connections* – Share your heart or play games with loved ones.
6. *Nutritious Food* – Choose whole, natural foods.
7. *Spiritual Growth* – Engage with a community or practice that aligns with your beliefs
8. *Intentional Rest* – Activities that renew and restore.
9. *Cold Baths and Sauna* – Improve sleep and refresh the body.
10. *Grounding* – Walk barefoot on grass or swim in the sea to connect with nature.

Sneaking in Good Habits – Through the Back Door of the Subconscious.

1. *Invest in a Better Tomorrow*

By taking small, consistent steps, you can establish healthy habits that become second nature over time.

2. *Set Yourself on "Cruise Control"*

Find balance where positive routines become automatic, requiring little conscious effort.

3. *Run Fast Enough to Leave Old Habits Behind*

Good habits will eventually feel harder to abandon than to maintain.

. . .

How to Identify the Right Habits:

1. What do you enjoy doing that others might find challenging?
2. What activities help you lose track of time?
3. Where do you naturally excel?
4. What skills come effortlessly to you?

Repetition – The Key to Success

- What am I doing well? Write down the good choices you make.
- What could I improve? Learn from your mistakes.
- What did I learn? Use your experiences as stepping stones for growth.

"Healing comes with attention." When we focus on our habits, we begin to see what builds us up and what tears us down. With clarity and intention, you can create a life rich in balance, joy, and growth.

Think Bigger – Step Out of Old Patterns

To recognize the chains that keep us bound to old habits, we must step out of the cultural conditioning we've adapted to.

- *See the Big Picture:* What influences your thoughts, behaviors, and decisions?
- *Run Fast Enough:* Breaking free from old habits requires energy and clarity—start by replacing one pattern at a time with a better choice.

———

Key Steps to Establish a New Habit:

1. *Set Goals:* Start with small, manageable changes.
2. *Repeat Daily:* Consistency strengthens new habits and weakens old patterns.
3. *Monitor Progress:* Keep track of what works and what needs adjustment.
4. *Cultivate Joy:* Focus on enjoying the journey rather than fixating on the end result.

Real Life Story: Transformation Through Small Steps

Luke felt constantly fatigued and found it difficult to change his routine. He started small—by placing his running shoes by his bed at night. The first step was simply putting on the shoes and stepping outside.

Gradually, he increased his activity and made running a daily habit. By planning ahead and taking small, steady steps, he achieved lasting change and significantly improved his quality of life.

Self-Reflecting Questions

1. What's preventing you from starting a new habit, and how can you reduce that barrier?
2. How might new habits positively impact your relationships?
3. What simple actions can you take today to ease the introduction of new habits?

Goals and Plans

Give a new habit 6–12 weeks to solidify. Once it's harder to skip than to do, introduce another habit.

By adding 4–6 habits each year, you can transform your life and achieve greater balance and well-being.

Answer the questions and meditate for 10 minutes. Reflect on what you are sensing after this work and write it down

Day 15

Neurotransmitters – How We Shape Our Well-being

This chapter explores the crucial role neurotransmitters play in mood and vitality, emphasizing small lifestyle adjustments—like exercise, healthy nutrition, and mindful habits—that foster mental and physical balance while steering life toward nourishment rather than numbing distractions.

Take a deep breath and meditate for 5 minutes

The Orchestra of Well-being

Neurotransmitters are like the musicians in an orchestra, each playing a unique role in creating harmony.

Serotonin sets the steady rhythm of contentment, dopamine provides bursts of excitement like a triumphant melody, endorphins offer the soothing tones that ease tension, and oxytocin adds warmth and connection, like the heartfelt strings.

For the orchestra to perform its best, it needs a skilled conductor—you. Through mindful habits like proper nutrition, movement, rest, and self-care, you can guide the musicians to play in harmony, creating a symphony of balance and vitality.

In day 5, "The mind", I focused on mastering my thoughts by breaking old patterns, practicing mindfulness, and developing new mental habits that help me stay present, find balance, and support my personal growth.

In day 10, "The brain", I focused on the importance of nurturing my brain through balanced routines, proper nutrition, rest, and exercise.

By taking small, intentional actions, I enhance my focus, clarity, and overall well-being, paving the way for transformative mental and physical health.

The nervous system is the ultimate prescription for health and vitality. Understanding Neurotransmitters:
The subconscious mind tends to mask the truth to maintain stability, often keeping us within our comfort zones even when they hinder progress. To counter this, it's essential to focus on improving lifestyle habits in small, consistent steps—without excessive expectations or harsh self-criticism.

Neurotransmitters influence our mood, energy, and how we perceive and experience life. They help us connect with others, enjoy life, and face challenges.

Maintaining a healthy balance of these chemicals through a mindful lifestyle routine fosters stability and well-being.

Our behaviors affect our bodies and neurotransmitters. Conscious changes in habits can transform our mental state and enhance our sense of well-being.

My Story

When I was a young man, I developed a need for: mind-altering consumption. I got lost in daydreams. I played slot machines. I used snuff and later nicotine pouches. I watched pornography. I drank alcohol. I played billiards and poker for money.

By the time I was 15, I had programmed my life around this behavior. It was a constant need—always something missing. My life was a prison of neurotransmitters, ruled by the scarcity monster.

What I didn't realize was those bad habits feed more bad habits. The body and mind crave more of what they already have.

In 1996, I went to rehab and stopped drinking. I started attending AA meetings, lifting weights, and meditating. I began hiking mountains, reading books, and swimming in the sea. I went back to school and landed my dream job. Good habits push out bad habits. Bad habits push out good habits.

Neurotransmitters

- Feeling good → Eat healthy food.
- Feeling bad → Turn to TV or other mind-altering distractions.
- News → Often fuels negativity.

My father always had a chronic cold during his final years of smoking.

- Chronic cold → Nicotine.
- Chronic headaches → Muscle tension.
- Chronic irritability → Sugar, yeast, wheat, caffeine, alcohol, unhealthy fats.
- Chronic fatigue → Alcohol, nicotine, sugar, fat.

Are you nourishing or depleting yourself? Tinker with the keyboard until you find the solution. The Other Side of the Coin: Throw away the keyboard and look for someone or something to blame.

Transformative elements

Lifestyle Habits and Their Impact

1. *Exercise* – Boosts mood and enhances well-being.

2. *Diet* – Vegetables, healthy fats, and nutrient-rich foods strengthen the body.
3. *Alcohol and Caffeine* – Can increase anxiety and stress when consumed excessively.
4. *Rest and Sleep* – Equally as important as work. Resting the mind improves decision-making and increases energy.

Think of the body like a geyser: if we constantly impose stress, it loses its power. We must nurture ourselves to maintain health and vitality.

Neurotransmitters and How to Support Them -
Serotonin – Mood and Stability

- *What helps?* Massage, outdoor activities, sunlight, meditation, journaling, healthy food, vitamin D, deep conversations, nature, and mindfulness exercises.

Dopamine – The Reward Neurotransmitter

- *What helps?* Achieving goals, exercise, good sleep, dancing, completing tasks, self-care, and exposure to daylight.

Endorphins – Natural Painkillers

- *What helps?* Cardio exercise, laughter, music, enjoyable activities, positive movies, sex, and dancing.

Oxytocin – The Love Hormone

- *What helps?* Hugs, physical touch, active listening,

petting animals, helping others, spending time with loved ones, and cuddling.

Reflections on Self-Care and Connection

1. *News: Nourish or Drain*

Every piece of information affects our well-being.
Choose news and content that uplifts you rather than drains you.

2. *Habits: Gift or Curse*

Your habits are either a gift that supports your future or a curse that holds you back.
Which habits are you cultivating today?

3. *Words and Thoughts*

The words you choose for yourself, and others shape your thoughts.
Each thought and word form a link in the chain of life.

4. *Who Leads Your Life?*

Who is the captain of your life—your environment and habits, or you?

5. *Starting Point*

Where do you begin? Your first step matters. It doesn't have to be perfect—just a start.

6. *The Song and Calm of the Nervous System*

Singing has a remarkable effect on the nervous system, calming the mind and connecting us to our hearts.

7. *True Listening*

Listening requires a genuine desire to understand, not just to respond or correct.

8. *Mirroring Your World*

The world reflects what we put out. Every interaction is a mirror of our thoughts and attitudes.

9. *The Greatest Gift*

Avoid being a "policeman" in relationships—connect with warmth and empathy, not to control or correct.

Tips and Insights

1. *Comfort, Learning, Panic*

Growth occurs on the edge of comfort and learning—not in panic. Find the balance.

2. *Ground Yourself*

Connect with nature—walk barefoot, swim in the sea, or spend time in greenery.

3. *A Joyful Heart*

Reflect on what fills your heart with joy and focus on doing more of it.

4. A Broken Circuit

If something within you isn't working, identify what needs repair. It could be neglected emotional wounds or unresolved issues.

5. A Mind Full of Clutter

Awareness can collect unhelpful thoughts and patterns. Find ways to release what no longer serves you.

The Levels of Distress

- *Hurt by Others:* If you feel bad, ask yourself: Who is creating this discomfort?
- *Talking About It:* Talk consciously about feelings to release them but avoid feeding negativity.

Guidance

Think about where you want to go, not just what you want to avoid. Balance acknowledging challenges with focusing on solutions.

Incorporating Change into Life - Ask yourself:

- What elements do I want to integrate into my daily life to improve my well-being?
- How can I create an environment that supports my mental and physical health?
- How can I foster greater emotional stability?
- How can I activate the feel-good hormones?
- Where can I find natural pain relief?
- How can I bring more warmth and kindness into my life?

Short-Term Solutions vs. Long-Term Challenges. Short-term fixes often provide momentary relief but lead to long-term discomfort. Here are examples:

1. *Numbing Emotions.*
   - Avoiding pain or problems with temporary distractions like unhealthy eating, screen time, or escapism.
   - This delays solutions and allows issues to grow.
2. *Need vs. Want.*
   - When we think we "need" something—recognition, possessions, or circumstances—we create unhealthy dependencies.
   - This need-based mindset fosters a sense of lack and a loss of control.
3. *Shutting Down.*
   - Not sharing feelings or needs can isolate us, leading to inner frustration and a tendency to numb rather than address issues.
4. *Draining vs. Nourishing Life.*
   - Living in a needy state keeps us searching for what's missing. This drains energy and prevents growth.
   - A nourishing life focuses on building what we have, creating stability and peace.

Key Steps for Change:

1. *Nourish Your Core.*
   - Healthy habits and thoughts strengthen your sense of self, making you more resilient to external pressures.
2. *Shift from Need to Want.*
   - A change in mindset is crucial. Wanting things

from a place of strength and intention is healthier than feeling dependent or lacking.
3. *Connect and Share.*
    - Sharing emotions, needs, and experiences opens space for connection and healing.
4. *Live in the Now.*
    - A nourishing life focuses on building on what you have now rather than chasing what you don't have. This creates balance and inner peace.

Reflection

What path do you take when seeking solutions to discomfort? Do you numb or nourish? Awareness of these decisions can change everything.

A Real-Life Story – Transformation

Marta struggled with insomnia and constant anxiety. She drank four cups of coffee daily and couldn't find time to exercise.

After learning about neurotransmitters, she made one small change—reducing her caffeine intake and starting a ten-minute daily walk.

Over time, she added deep breathing exercises and began writing gratitude notes each evening. These small adjustments helped her sleep better and feel calmer. She noticed positive changes in her mood and energy.

Self-Reflecting Questions

1. What lifestyle changes could you make to improve your well-being?

2. Which neurotransmitters do you feel are lacking in your life, and what changes could help boost them?

3. How can you implement small, realistic changes that support your mental and physical health?

Closing Words

If we think of our body as the hot spring Geysir, people once started putting soap into it to force it to erupt. Now, it no longer erupts. Similarly, if we continuously force our bodies with constant stress and stimuli, they lose their strength. We need to nurture ourselves to maintain health and well-being.

Answer the questions and meditate for 10 minutes. Reflect on what you are sensing after this work and write it down

Day 16

Understanding the World Better – The Value of Reading and Inner Peace

This chapter emphasizes the transformative power of reading and meaningful connections in combating modern distractions, fostering self-awareness, and nurturing emotional well-being through genuine relationships and reflective practices.

> *Take a deep breath and meditate for 5 minutes*

The Mirror and the Window

Reading and meaningful connections are like a mirror and a window.

Books act as a mirror, reflecting your thoughts, emotions, and inner struggles, helping you see yourself more clearly.

At the same time, meaningful discussions are like a window, opening your perspective to the world and allowing you to connect deeply with others.

Both tools help you escape the confines of distraction and isolation, fostering self-awareness, inner peace, and a richer understanding of life.

In day 6, "Building a new personality", I delved into how becoming more self-aware, confronting my inner struggles, and embracing new experiences can help me transform old patterns, cultivate inner prosperity, and bring harmony to both my mind and body.

In day 11, "The journey", I see life as a transformative journey of growth, learning, and evolution.

By letting go of resistance, embracing change, and nurturing my self-awareness, I move toward balance, peace, and meaningful progress.

My Story – Connection, The Key to Emotional and Mental Well-being

One evening, my wife came home late, exhausted, to find the dinner I had prepared for her. Frustrated, I demanded answers and insisted on keeping the food warm while waiting for her.

My sense of imbalance and need for fairness led me to scold her. She broke into tears, and the evening was ruined.

This story highlights how perception and understanding can shape interactions and resolve conflicts.

> As Albert Einstein once said:
> *"You perceive more than you understand."*

By being attuned to her exhaustion, I could have recognized that this was not the time to demand accountability.
Despite my intuition, frustration took over,
resulting in unnecessary pain and a ruined evening.

Lessons Learned:

1. *Read the Situation:* Meeting others where they are can be more important than demanding what we feel is fair.
2. *Manage Personal Reactions:* Address your feelings before they affect others.
3. *Create Space for Connection:* Instead of pushing for resolutions, offer understanding and compassion.

This incident underscores the importance of intuition in guiding interactions.

Listening to intuition rather than impulsive emotions can strengthen relationships instead of damaging them.

Transformative elements

The Power of Reading

> George Orwell once said:
> "The best books... are those that tell you what you already know."

In a world dominated by noise and distractions, reading offers a chance to clarify our thoughts and enhance our awareness.

Technology often diminishes our ability to be present, drawing us into unhealthy entertainment that drains rather than nourishes us.

The Effects of Modern Entertainment

- *Time-consuming distractions:* Scrolling, watching, and getting lost in virtual realities often leave us feeling empty.
- *Screen-induced fatigue:* Blue light disrupts sleep and impairs our ability to recharge.
- *Erosion of connections:* Activities like excessive use of porn and social isolation disrupt healthy relationships and commitment.

On the other hand, reading fosters deeper connections with ourselves and the world. Books by authors like Jhon Irving and Barbara Fisher that have deep insights into the human nature, reflecting our emotions and relationships.

Jón Kalman beautifully captures this in his writing:
"*The saddest thing about humans is that they never escape themselves.*"

Through literature, we can explore ourselves through the lens of others and deepen our understanding of emotions and relationships.

Discussions and Connections: Finding Value in Conversations

Socrates emphasized:
"*But I say, however, that the best thing for a person is to engage in daily discussions about virtue and to examine both oneself and others, for an unexamined life is not worth living. Nevertheless, this is the way things are now, and it is no easy task to convince others of this.*"

The Power of Meaningful Connections

As Proverbs reminds us:
"*As iron sharpens iron, so one person sharpens another.*"

Who in your life nurtures your growth and strengthens your inner peace? Cultivating connections with those who help us grow and reflect on ourselves is invaluable.

Just as our bodies need nourishing food, our spirits require meaningful conversations. Speaking with a trusted friend or counsellor can unlock deeper self-awareness and emotional growth.

In today's society, where many turn to virtual worlds for connection, the importance of genuine relationships has never been greater.

Presence, listening, and collaboration give us the strength to navigate life's challenges and find purpose.

. . .

Reflection Questions

1. Who in your life helps you grow and enhances your emotional well-being?
2. How can you nurture these connections further?

When Mindfulness Flows Best

- If you think of someone, what does it mean?
- If you dream of someone, could it be a sign to reconnect?
- Listening to your awareness opens doors to deeper understanding.

Our thoughts shape sparks of connection. What you think governs how you feel, and unspoken thoughts often lead to ill-considered words.

Society and Social Isolation

A lifestyle centered on isolation, screens, and TV increases social distance.

The younger generation faces the effects of violent virtual realities, which can negatively impact society, including rising aggression.

To combat this, we must emphasize deep connections and open ourselves to being presentfor one another.

A Real-Life Story: Finding Inner Peace Through Reading

Jakob was a man always on the go. His days were consumed by work, and his evenings were spent scrolling on his phone or watching TV, leaving him feeling unrested.

One day, he decided to read a book recommended by a friend.

Starting with just 10 minutes of reading each night before bed, he noticed a sense of calm and clarity.

Over time, reading became a habit that allowed him to explore new perspectives and learn about himself through the stories of others.

Gradually, he reduced his screen time and found balance and peace by focusing on activities that nourished him.

Self-Reflecting Questions

1. What changes might occur if you incorporated reading or deeper conversations into your daily life?
2. How can you create more meaningful connections with yourself and others instead of falling into shallow distractions?
3. Which book has had the most impact on you, and how has it shaped your worldview?

Final Words

Understanding the world better begins with self-reflection and connection with others.

Through reading, discussions, and genuine relationships, we can discover greater peace, joy, and understanding of ourselves and the world.

Sharing is healing. If you don't share, you close yourself off.

Belonging quiets the inner critic and fosters harmony within.

Answer the questions and meditate for 10 minutes. Reflect on what you are sensing after this work and write it down

Day 17

The Judge – A Journey to Compassion and Self-Understanding

This chapter explores the pervasive presence of the inner judge in our lives, offering tools and reflections to transform harsh self-criticism and judgment into compassion, self-awareness, and understanding, ultimately fostering deeper connections with ourselves and others.

Take a deep breath and meditate for 5 minutes

The Shadow on the Wall

The inner judge is like a shadow cast on a wall, larger and darker than the reality it reflects. It follows us, pointing out flaws and mistakes, making us feel trapped in its presence.

But the shadow is not the truth—it is simply the result of light hitting our fears and insecurities. By turning toward the light —compassion, self-awareness, and understanding—we diminish the shadow's power and see ourselves as we truly are: human, imperfect, and deserving of grace.

In day 7, "The 5% syndrome", I dive into the concept of my internal "operating system," uncovering how outdated habits and recurring thought patterns consume 95% of my mental energy.

By taking actionable steps, I learn to redesign this system, creating a more conscious, balanced, and fulfilling life.

In day 12, "Are you free or a prisoner", I reflect on my journey from self-imposed emotional imprisonment—shaped by past traumas and fear of others' opinions—to the freedom I've found through self-acceptance, forgiveness, and living in alignment with my own values.

> "It's easy to judge. It's more difficult to understand. Understanding requires compassion, patience, and a willingness to believe that good hearts sometimes choose poor methods."
> – Sadia Psychology

What does the mental "tape" in your head sound like when you wake up? For many, the "judge" takes control immediately – the tapes start spinning: *"Why didn't I go to bed earlier?" "Why did I eat that?" "I'm still too fat."*

This inner voice can be harsh and relentless, often reflecting the environment we grew up in.

We all have an inner judge – a voice that criticizes, evaluates, and passes judgment on both ourselves and others. This judge often originates from past experiences and the values we were raised with. It can trap us in negative thought patterns and distrust.

Becoming aware of this judge and learning to quiet it can help us live freer lives with more compassion.

My Story

It was a workday at the preschool where I worked, and everyone was excited about an ATV ride on the schedule.

Before we started, we received clear instructions: if we drove the ATV into water and made it inoperable, we would face a hefty fine.

Wanting to impress my colleagues, I floored the gas. Despite never having driven an ATV before, I wanted to prove myself. Before I knew it, the ATV was submerged in a large puddle and wouldn't start.

I felt an overwhelming sense of shame – more than I had ever felt before. The shame was so intense I couldn't endure it.

At the time, I had no money and wasn't in a good place. I turned my defense into offense, blamed others for the mistake, denied responsibility, and acted immaturely. I hit rock bottom, unable to manage the situation.

Transformative elements

Training to Address the Inner Judge

- *Self-Reflection*

When the critical voice begins, pause and observe without judgment. Ask yourself:
"What is happening inside me right now?"

- *Compassion and Forgiveness*

By showing yourself and others compassion, you reduce the judge's influence. Remember, criticism often leads to tension, while compassion and understanding alleviate it.

- *Letting Go of Perfectionism*

Avoid trying to control every situation. Allow yourself to be a witness rather than the director of the stage.

- *Choosing Your Role*

Do you want to be a witness who observes or a high priest who tries to control everything? This decision can shift your perspective on yourself and others.

. . .

The Origin of the Judge

Growing up, I was surrounded by an environment of clear opinions and prejudice against other groups and perspectives.

The world was described as harsh, the weather bad, and the news filled with negativity. The saying *"What the young learn, the old practice"* describes this well.

I internalized these ideas, embedding them in my mental operating system. Without realizing it, I became full of judgment, both toward myself and others.

This limited my possibilities, reduced my quality of life, and kept me trapped in critical patterns. Today, I work to recognize and stop the judge. When I notice it taking over, I press a mental "stop" button – sometimes literally tapping my chest.

This simple practice helps me silence the judge and choose compassion and understanding instead.

Becoming a Witness, Not a Director

> *"We rarely love virtues we do not ourselves possess."*
> – William Shakespeare.

The judge seeks culprits, but this book – this path – isn't about finding them. It's about seeing things as they are, without judgment.

> The gospel says in Matthew 7:1-2
> *"Do not judge, or you too will be judged. For in the same way you judge others, you will be judged, and with the measure you use, it will be measured to you."*

When we judge others, we often reflect our own state of being.

We shine a spotlight on others' flaws while needing a magnifying glass to see our own. It's far easier to look outward than inward.

Forgive or Forsake

Forgiveness doesn't change the past, but it expands the future.

We are often quick to forgive those who speak ill of us but struggle to forgive those we have spoken ill of. Why is that?

We may forgive those who irritate us but find it harder to forgive those who think we are irritating. *"Those who forgive most are forgiven the most."*

Forgiveness is a measure of the love in our hearts. We forgive to the extent that we love.

Reflections on "Red Flags" in Life

We often hear about discrepancies between words and actions. When I look back, there were countless red flags I ignored. The question I had to ask myself was: *Why?*

I was most vulnerable to what I lacked. What I felt I was missing became an infinite need.

This need, rooted in the past, shaped my perspective. The red flags – the warnings – were lost in the fog of my pain. I didn't see situations as they were; I saw them through the lens of my wounds.

When the healing process began, it was instinctive to point fingers at others – to direct attention outward. I couldn't bear the weight of facing what had transpired in my life.

This process took time, and with each step, I learned more about myself and my inner world.

Key Points on the Journey

1. *Identifying the Problem* - Finding a new motivator to take the next step forward.

2. *Living in Anticipation* - Putting yourself in a mindset of openness to what comes, without creating expectations that burden the heart.

3. *Repetition Over Experience* - What we do regularly becomes ingrained habits that can either build us up or keep us trapped.

The Path Forward

When we learn to acknowledge the red flags instead of ignoring them, new understanding opens up. We better comprehend where we come from, why we reacted a certain way, and how to make better choices in the future.

Moving from living with expectations to living in anticipation allows us to let go of pain and open our hearts to what truly matters.

Exercise: Growing Beyond the Judge - "Through judging, we separate. Through understanding, we grow."

When you feel the judge awakening, ask yourself:

- What is happening inside me right now?

- Why is this feeling or thought arising?

- What would change if I didn't engage with judgment but simply observed it?

———

Self-Reflecting Questions

1. What situations trigger the judge in you, and how do you respond?
2. How can you work with your inner judge to transform criticism into understanding and compassion?
3. What small changes can you make to be a witness rather than a director in your life?

Final Words

"If your foot slips, it's easily corrected, but if your tongue slips, it may be irreparable."
– Benjamin Franklin

Step out of the role of the judge to help those who have fallen. One of the greatest opportunities to do good is to support those the world judges most harshly. Our closest people may need us the most when they least deserve it.

The judge is a part of us all, but we decide whether it rules. By practicing being a witness, we can unlock the doors to compassion, freedom, and deeper connections with ourselves and others.

What can you do today to break the judge's patterns and choose understanding over harshness?

Answer the questions and meditate for 10 minutes. Reflect on what you are sensing after this work and write it down

Day 18

Active with Yourself" – The Journey from Co-dependence to Self-Respect

In this chapter we move from co-dependency to self-respect. It is a transformative journey of self-awareness, setting boundaries, and embracing one's authentic self. Through conscious decisions and introspection, we learn to balance helping others with maintaining our own peace and integrity.

Take a deep breath and meditate for 5 minutes

The Balancing Act

Imagine yourself as a tightrope walker. On one side lies codependence—a pull toward pleasing others, sacrificing your balance to meet their needs.

On the other side is isolation—detaching entirely to protect yourself. The path to self-respect lies in walking the rope with steady steps, guided by boundaries and authentic self-awareness.

In day 8, "Communication", I explore how practicing mindful communication—grounded in respect, understanding, and self-awareness—helps me foster stronger connections, support emotional growth, and cultivate inner peace.

By focusing on building bridges instead of walls, I nurture healthier and more meaningful relationships.

In day 13, "Embracing what is", I explore the importance of appreciating the present, releasing old patterns, and nurturing love and respect in my relationships.

These are the keys to finding inner peace and experiencing true happiness.

"Active with Yourself" – The Journey from Co-dependence to Self-Respect. *"The rarest gem is peace; I would give everything for it, except the truth."*

Peace and truth are the foundations of self-understanding and connection to oneself.

But how can we achieve peace in a world that often values pleasing others over being true to ourselves?

My Story - Using Anger to Transform My Life

In 2003, at the age of 29, I was walking down Skútuvogur Street when a thought hit me like a hammer:

"I am addicted to pleasing others and rejecting myself." The realization filled me with anger—a productive anger. I couldn't bear the idea of living a life prioritizing others at the expense of my own well-being.

At that time, I was working two jobs under domineering bosses.

I constantly sought their approval, flattering them and proving myself to them. One of them even nicknamed me "Little Bubbi," a label that deepened my pain. *I knew I couldn't live like this anymore.*

The Path to Change. I decided to take control of my life and attended CoDA (Codependents Anonymous) meetings. These meetings taught me to work through the 12 steps and helped me rebuild my self-respect and confidence.

In time, I even found humor in my bosses' behavior, seeing them in a new light. They no longer held power over me.

The Washing Machine – A Symbol of Transformation

During this period, I needed a new washing machine. A friend suggested buying a used one, but something within me rebelled: *"No! I deserve a new washing machine!"* This wasn't just about an appliance—it was a declaration of my worth.

Harnessing Anger as a Driving Force
I learned to channel anger, not as a destructive force but as fuel for change. It pushed me to step out of the cycle of people-pleasing and reclaim my life.

I also began organizing new CoDA meetings, helping others work through the steps as I had.

My life began to flourish as I learned to trust my own voice, respect my needs, and grow.

Lessons from Co-dependence
"There is no shame in recognizing patterns that diminish you. The courage to face and transform them leads to real growth."

By acknowledging my worth and taking responsibility for my life, I unlocked possibilities I hadn't seen before.

A Lesson in Helping Without Losing Yourself:
In 2012, I tried to make a positive impact on others.

I visited a taxi station, put up posters, and offered free sessions in my wellness studio to over 100 drivers. No one came. Later, I heard one of the drivers had to be rescued from his car by a fire engine due to health issues. I realized then: *good intentions alone aren't enough.*

The Lesson on Co-dependence
This experience taught me an essential truth: co-dependence is learned helplessness. It is the tendency to try to save others, even when they are not ready to help themselves.

My desire to help was strong, but it was not aligned with their own willingness or ability to address their problems.

Understanding this imbalance between intention and reality

was a pivotal step in recognizing the boundaries needed for healthy relationships.

True support comes not from fixing others but from empowering them to take responsibility for their own growth and challenges.

Transformative elements

Self-Reflection

1. *Why is saying "no" so difficult for me?*
   - Am I afraid of rejection, loss, or disappointing others?
2. *Why do I feel uncomfortable when I stand up for myself?*
   - Have I grown accustomed to prioritizing others' needs over my own?
3. *What fears are tied to being authentically myself?*
   - Who taught me that I am not enough as I am?

Steps Toward Balance

1. *Learn to Say "No"*
   - Practice saying "no" with kindness but firmness. Remember: saying "no" to one thing is saying "yes" to something else that matters to you.
2. *Stand Up for Yourself:*
   - Each time you advocate for yourself, you strengthen your self-respect. If discomfort follows, ask: "Is this feeling based on real consequences or old patterns?"
3. *Differentiate Between Love and Co-dependence:*

- Love allows space and respect, while co-dependence diminishes you by sacrificing your balance for others' approval.
4. *Break the Spiral of Endless Mental Conversations:*
    - Notice how much energy you spend imagining what to say. Ask yourself: "What if I were simply honest?"
5. *Listen to Your Body:*
    - Physical pain can often signal unresolved emotions. Pause and reflect: "What is my body trying to tell me?"
6. *Speak Your Mind:*
    - Practice expressing yourself without fear. Start with small things and grow your confidence in your own voice.

What Is Co-dependence?

Co-dependence is like an invisible hat many wear unknowingly. It manifests in various ways:

- Struggling to say "no".
- Feeling worse after standing up for oneself.
- Difficulty being authentic out of fear of others' reactions.
- Neglecting one's own needs to please others.
- Discomfort with setting boundaries.

It's a state where we lose connection with ourselves and allow others' emotions to dictate our well-being.

The Unholy Trinity

1. *The "me" I am not allowed to be.*
2. *The "me" I try to be but cannot sustain.*

3. *The "me" I should be but never feel I am.*

This trinity represents the inner conflicts co-dependence creates. It causes us to lose our voice, please others, and disconnect from our own needs. *Key Takeaways:*

1. *Help Requires Willingness*
   - People must be ready to take steps for themselves. You cannot save someone unwilling to help themselves.
2. *Give Without Expectations*
   - Offering help, is valuable, regardless of whether others accept it.
3. *Guard Against Co-dependence*
   - Co-dependence often involves solving others' problems at your expense. Healthy boundaries are essential.

This experience taught me the importance of balance in helping others without losing myself.
Despite No One Accepting the Offer, a Lesson in Balance.
This experience opened my eyes to the importance of finding balance in helping others without taking responsibility for their problems.
Sometimes, the best way to help is by allowing others to take their own steps forward.

What No One Can Take Away from You – The Core of Life
In life, the most important work is building what no one can take away from you: your mindset, character, personality, transparency, and entire being. These are the foundations that not only define us as individuals but also guide us toward deeper well-being and balance.

. . .

Time, the Heart, and Behavior

- *Time* determines the people you will meet along life's journey.
- *The heart* decides whom you wish to invite into your life.
- *Your behavior* determines who stays as part of it.

When we muster the courage to say goodbye to what no longer serves us—whether toxic ideas, bad habits, or mismatched relationships—new doors open, and life rewards us with fresh opportunities.

Chaos and Change

Chaos is not merely physical disorder. It encompasses old patterns, toxic relationships, and ideas that keep us stuck rather than supporting the best version of ourselves.

As Elanor Brown aptly put it:
"Clutter is anything that doesn't support your better self."

Acknowledging Inner Struggles

The wise recognize their inner struggles and take responsibility for them. They understand that solutions begin within.

The unwise, on the other hand, constantly seek scapegoats and blame others for their problems. Michael Meade captures this truth perfectly: *"The wise learn to know their inner conflicts, while the unwise blame others for all their troubles."* By reflecting on these lessons, we create a pathway toward growth, self-awareness, and harmony in both our inner and outer worlds.

———

Key Steps Toward Self-Awareness and Balance:

1. *Acknowledge What No Longer Serves You.*

Take a close look at relationships, habits, and ideas that hold you back. Recognize what keeps you from moving forward.

2. *Cultivate What No One Can Take Away.*

Focus on building your inner strength, self-confidence, and integrity. These qualities form the foundation of lasting self-respect and fulfillment.

3. *Be Mindful of Those You Choose to Let into Your Life.*

The people and relationships you allow in shape your experiences and outlook. Choose carefully—what you permit influences who you become.

4. *Clear the Chaos.*

Let go of old, outdated thoughts, habits, and attachments. By creating space for new energy, you open the door to growth and renewal.

Life is a blend of our inner state and the external decisions we make By focusing on what no one can take away—our mindset, integrity, and self-worth—we establish the foundation for a life of balance, purpose, and inner peace.
Reflections on Co-dependence

- *"If I carry the emotions of others, there is no space for my own."* Co-dependence can rob us of the emotional room to process and honor our own feelings.

- *"The one who dares not say what they think will eventually think differently than what they say."* Suppressing your truth to please others leads to internal conflict and a loss of authenticity.
- *"We stop being ourselves and transform into what we think others want us to be."* This constant reshaping leaves us disconnected from our true selves and prevents genuine connection with others.

By acknowledging and addressing these patterns, we can step away from co-dependence and cultivate a life rooted in self-awareness, authenticity, and meaningful relationships.

Healing Steps Toward Self-Respect:

1. *Acknowledge Pain and Hopelessness*
   - Facing what causes distress is the first step to learning from it.
2. *Set Boundaries*
   - Boundaries preserve self-respect and peace.
3. *Choose Growth Over Comfort*
   - Avoid environments of drama, dishonesty, or disrespect.

A Practice: Who Controls You?

1. Ask yourself: *Who in my life influences my decisions the most?*
2. Choose to step out of the role of caretaker and embrace independence.
3. Practice setting and maintaining boundaries.

Final Words

Breaking free from co-dependence is a journey that requires courage, introspection, and a willingness to change. It's about acknowledging your needs, setting healthy boundaries, and stepping out of patterns that hold you back.

By choosing peace over drama, self-respect over people-pleasing, and healthy communication over denial, you can create a life of inner balance and tranquility.

Answer the questions and meditate for 10 minutes. Reflect on what you are sensing after this work and write it down

Day 19

Core Values – The Foundation of Well-being and Decisions

In this chapter we explore the role of core values in shaping decisions, fostering balance, and creating a purposeful life, emphasizing honesty, family, and respect as essential pillars for personal growth and well-being.

Take a deep breath and meditate for 5 minutes

"Core values are the compass of our lives; they point us toward true north, ensuring that even in the storms of uncertainty, we navigate with purpose and integrity."

In day 4, "Health Box", I learned a balanced environment that nourishes both my body and mind. By cultivating intentional habits, practicing self-respect, and removing distractions, I enable myself to grow and embrace simplicity.

In day 9, "The Energy", I delve into the importance of managing and directing my energy—spiritual, mental, emotional, and physical.

By focusing on what nourishes me rather than what depletes me, I work to build balance, break cycles of fatigue, and create a fulfilling life.

In day 14, "Habits and lifestyle development", I reflect on the role of habits in shaping my life.

By using practical strategies to create supportive routines, build self-awareness, and introduce positive habits through small, consistent steps, I work toward lasting balance and personal growth.

> "People often say this or that person has yet to find themselves. But the self is not something one finds; it is something one creates."
> – Thomas S. Szasz, Hungarian American professor

Our core values represent life in its simplest form. They drive our decisions, changes, and how we perceive the world.

When we live in alignment with our values, we find balance and inner peace. These values are a guiding light, helping us make clear decisions and leading us toward a life that reflects our inner truth.

My Story – Truth, an Uncompromising Value

> "The truth you hesitate to accept is the foundation of your liberation."
> – Joseph Campbell

As a teenager, I spent most of my time in a billiard hall. It was a gathering place for all the lost boys.

Our lives revolved around having money, getting drunk, and pursuing girls. We all carried deep insecurities, often expressed as verbal abuse – a way to cope with our inferiority complex. Lies were a routine part of our lives.

We constantly gambled for money, whether at billiards or poker. When I had money, life felt good, but without it, life was unbearable. Everything was sacrificed in pursuit of cash. We forged checks and stole whatever we could. Lies became our daily bread, keeping the charade alive.

When I finally started addressing my issues and began telling the truth, I felt the tangible power of honesty. No longer having to revise what I could say or maintain falsehoods was liberating.

Since that time, truth has been a non-negotiable value in my life. Even today, I feel immense freedom in having nothing to hide.

If you work for the CIA, they scrutinize every aspect of your life to ensure no enemy can leverage an inconvenient truth against you. This underscores the power of truth – it can provide both freedom and protection from internal and external threats.

Transformative elements

What Are Core Values?

1. *Beliefs and Convictions*

Our values shape how we view the world and what we believe we can or cannot achieve. They often arise from decisions made in response to our experiences.

2. *Personal, Yet Not Absolute Truths*

They reflect our internal experiences but are not necessarily universal truths. Values are deeply individual and serve as the foundation of our personal perspective on life.

3. *Anchors in Thought Patterns*

Values act as anchors that support our thought patterns. They provide stability and frame our decisions and attitudes.

How Values Work for Us
Values serve as a catalyst for change. When we live in harmony with them, our well-being increases. Conversely, when our behavior contradicts our values, it can lead to conflict or dissatisfaction.

1. *Questions for Reflection:*
   - Is this working for me?
   - How could I do this differently?
   - What happens if I do nothing about this?

Plato once said: *"If you organize your life around higher values, everything else will follow naturally."*

Discovering Your Core Values

What are your top three values? Examples of values might include:

- Family
- Honesty
- Respect

Defining your own values is essential to building a strong character and a clear life direction. Values can be diverse and unique to everyone.

Meditation and Values

Reviewing your values and incorporating them into meditation can be powerful. Reflecting on values helps clarify what truly matters and strengthens your connection with yourself.

Meditation guide for values:

1. Find a quiet space.
2. Take deep breaths and relax your body.
3. Reflect on one value at a time – what does it mean to you?
4. Ask yourself: How do my values manifest in my daily life?

Examples: Family, Honesty, and Respect

Discovering which values matter most to you is crucial for shaping a strong character. Values can vary widely and are deeply personal.

1. Family

Family is often considered a top priority, offering a sense of security and belonging. Having a loving family, you can trust and turn to provides stability, joy, and comfort.

However, family also comes with responsibilities. You get what you give.

If you feel a lack of love or care, ask yourself if you're giving what you wish to receive. Love is a privilege that requires constant nurturing. It is not automatic and demands effort. Like a waterfall that never stops flowing – when you give love to others, you receive it yourself.

2. Honesty

Honesty is the foundation of any healthy life. Being true to yourself and others allows you to live in harmony and alignment.

Dishonesty, on the other hand, is like a complicated snare – constantly being on guard, fearing exposure. This creates unnecessary stress on your nervous system and affects those around you.

True words are alive. Speaking the truth and being honest deepens connections with others and strengthens your relationship with yourself.

Never underestimate your intuition – it guides you well.

Being true to yourself is an inexhaustible source of energy and happiness.

You don't have to hide anything, and you gain
the freedom to be your authentic self in all aspects of life.

. . .

3. Respect

Respect, both for yourself and others, is key to balance. Self-respect involves knowing and maintaining your boundaries.

While challenging at times, it's necessary to protect your physical, mental, and emotional health.

Respect also applies to how you interact with others.

Being around self-centered individuals who focus only on themselves can feel like sitting in a mud puddle – no one benefits.

However, by modeling respect and communication, you can help create healthier and deeper relationships.

A Real-Life Story: The Power of Honesty

Rut struggled with being honest in her relationships. She feared hurting others or causing disappointment. This fear led her to agree to things she cared deeply about but was unwilling to express.

One day, she realized this behavior was draining her energy. She decided to take small steps – being honest about simpler things, like what she wanted to eat or how she wanted to spend her free time.

Gradually, she succeeded in being truthful with herself and others.

At first, it was uncomfortable, but soon she noticed her connections with others became deeper and less strained.

The energy once spent maintaining a facade was now used to build confidence and relationships. Honesty became her guiding value, leading her to stability and well-being.

Self-Reflecting Questions

1. What does your family provide for you, and how can you contribute to strengthening those relationships?

2. What situations in your life call for greater honesty, both with yourself and others?
3. How can you build self-respect by setting boundaries or making decisions aligned with your values?

Closing Words

When we live in alignment with our values, we open the door to a life that is balanced, purposeful, and full of growth.

Values are not just guiding lights but the foundation for all our decisions. By working with them, defining them, and living by them, we achieve freedom and inner strength.

Answer the questions and meditate for 10 minutes. Reflect on what you are sensing after this work and write it down

Day 20

The Body – The Foundation of Well-Being and Balance

Chapter 20 emphasizes the vital role of nurturing the body through movement, nutrition, rest, and mindfulness, highlighting how healthy physical habits create a foundation for mental clarity, emotional balance, and overall well-being.

Take a deep breath and meditate for 5 minutes

The Foundation of Well-Being and Balance
"The body is like the foundation of a house; when cared for and strengthened, it supports everything above it, providing stability and resilience to weather life's storms."

In day 5, "The mind", I focus on mastering my thoughts by breaking old patterns, practicing mindfulness, and developing new mental habits that help me stay present, find balance, and support my personal growth.

In day 10, "The brain", I focus on the importance of nurturing my brain through balanced routines, proper nutrition, rest, and exercise.

By taking small, intentional actions, I enhance my focus, clarity, and overall well-being, paving the way for transformative mental and physical health.

In day 15, "Neurotransmitters", I explore the crucial role neurotransmitters play in my mood and vitality, focusing on how small lifestyle adjustments—like regular exercise, healthy nutrition, and mindful habits—help me foster mental and physical balance while guiding my life toward nourishment rather than numbing distractions.

The physical form seeps into the personal form

The body isn't just a vehicle; it's the foundation for quality of life, mental clarity, and overall well-being.

When we nurture our body, we enhance self-confidence, strengthen the mind, and release toxins that create internal stress.

By treating the body with care and respect, we empower both it and the mind to perform at their best, making daily life easier and more fulfilling.

My Story

As a young boy, I had habits that seemed trivial at the time but left lasting effects. I loved mayonnaise and rarely drank water.

These patterns followed me into adulthood, and at 51, I still struggle to drink enough water.

My body, shaped by years of habit, often craves foods I know aren't beneficial.

Similarly, I never developed the discipline to study at home. I would sit with the intention of learning but lacked the tools to follow through.

This pattern repeated itself in school, where I often failed, feeling trapped in a cycle I didn't know how to break.

These experiences taught me that childhood habits and routines echo far into adulthood. Rewiring those deep-seated patterns requires effort and self-awareness.

Today, I'm actively working to reprogram these habits—step by step. It's a journey, not a destination, and I'm finally ready to embrace it.

———

Transformative elements

Mindfulness and Connecting with the Body

Listening to the body and observing its signals can reveal inner needs. Emotions act as the body's vocabulary, offering clues about where attention and care are needed.

Practical Tips for Nurturing the Body and Mind:

1. *Routine and Movement*
   - Regular exercise improves flexibility, strength, and overall well-being. Simple activities like walking, stretching, or rowing can relieve tension and rejuvenate both body and mind.
   - Building 1 kg of muscle mass increases daily calorie burn by 30–50 calories.
2. *Sleep*
   - Poor sleep reduces metabolic efficiency and impacts focus. Consistent sleep routines enhance mental clarity and mood.
3. *Nutrition*
   - Choose nourishing, whole foods. Avoid sugar and unhealthy fats, as they directly affect health and emotional balance.
4. *Rest and Relaxation*
   - Deliberate rest, such as meditation or deep breathing, allows the body to recover and recharge.
5. *Attention and Intention*
   - Just as a well-maintained house requires upkeep, the body thrives on care and attention. Mindful

practices reinforce this maintenance and keep the body in its best shape.

The Link Between Physical and Mental Well-Being:

1. *Sleep*
    - Regular sleep patterns enhance metabolic efficiency and mental focus.
2. *Muscle Balance*
    - 80% of back pain stems from muscle imbalances.
3. *Nutrition and Cravings*
    - The body craves what it's accustomed to. Unhealthy foods can lead to cycles of cravings and guilt.
4. *Exercise Benefits*
    - Reduces blood pressure.
    - Strengthens heart chambers and improves cardiovascular efficiency.
    - Enhances capillary growth in muscles, aiding recovery and endurance.
    - Builds stronger bones and tendons.
    - Improves sleep, mood, and cognitive function.
    - Increases oxygen uptake and energy levels.

Toxins and Their Impact

Unhealthy food and lifestyle choices accumulate toxins that create stress and disrupt well-being. When the body is out of balance, the mind suffers too.

- A healthy body fosters a healthy mind.
- Balanced nutrition, rest, and exercise improve both physical and mental health.

Why Do I Shift into Neutral?
Sometimes we feel as though our body is working against us

rather than with us. It's as if something has shifted the gearstick into neutral, leaving us feeling stuck.

Our physical energy and balance dictate how we face the world—whether we can be present and channel our energy into actively participating in life.

The Body's Energy Levels – The Key to Balance

The body's energy levels govern our balance and our ability to engage with the present moment. It acts as the driver of our journey, and when we care for it properly, life becomes much smoother.

The body is our home, and how we treat it determines its stability. Proper care helps us maintain steady footing, even when life challenges us. *The hole we keep falling into is called imbalance.*

When Tension Becomes Too Much

The body has its limits. If we run it at high revs for too long—like a car stuck at 6000 RPM—we risk burnout.

"Too much tension that tries to burn everything" is a sign that we need to slow down, reevaluate our routines, and restore energy balance.

What does intentional rest look like to you?

Intentional rest is the foundation of the body's renewal.

It's not just about sleep but also mindful breathing, moments of presence, and calm intervals that allow the body to recover and rebalance.

What Are You "Downloading" Into Your Body?

The body craves what it's familiar with—whether good or bad habits. How you treat it determines how it responds:

- What is the current state of your body?

- What are your daily habits?

- Is your body the servant of your mind, or has it taken control?

The Interplay of Body and Mind

If thoughts are the vocabulary of the mind, emotions are the vocabulary of the body.

Your body communicates with you in its own way: through energy, discomfort, or well-being.

Your reactions and abilities are often in sync with the state of your body.

Like a machine, the body requires maintenance and fuel that supports its function.

Practical Steps to Address Neutral Mode:

1. *Evaluate Your Habits*

Take stock of your daily routines and identify what drains or nourishes your body.

2. *Prioritize Rest*

Incorporate deliberate moments of rest, such as meditation, slow breathing, or quiet reflection.

3. *Listen to Your Body's Signals*

Pay attention to energy levels, physical sensations, and any signs of imbalance or discomfort.

4. *Fuel Wisely*

Choose foods, movements, and environments that replenish rather than deplete your energy.

Your body is your lifelong partner. When you treat it with respect and care, it will serve you well, empowering you to navigate life with balance, energy, and presence.

The Body as Resistance: "The North remembers."
Sometimes, our mind knows what needs to be done, but the body resists. This creates a disconnect—like forgetting the "PIN code" to your health.

The body demands what it's used to, shaping habits that either serve or hinder us.

Reflection Questions

1. Is your body serving your mind, or has it taken control?
2. What daily habits are you reinforcing?
3. How do you maintain balance between body and mind?

A Story of Alignment
Once, a man forgot his PIN code but realized that the body remembers better than the mind.

Even though he hadn't written it down, his hands instinctively moved to the correct keys on the keypad. The body had learned the pattern.

This reminds us that the body remembers things the mind forgets—it stores emotions, habits, and behaviors that shape how we feel.

If we ignore these signals, the body may respond with discomfort or pain. However, if we listen to it and work in harmony with it, the body can thrive.

Actionable Steps for Physical and Mental Wellness

1. *Daily Movement*
   - Incorporate simple exercises or stretches into your routine.
2. *Healthy Eating*
   - Opt for nourishing foods and limit processed or sugary options.
3. *Quality Rest*
   - Prioritize deep, restorative sleep and incorporate mindful breaks during the day.
4. *Mindful Maintenance*
   - Treat your body like a valued home, ensuring it's cared for and respected.

Self-Reflecting Questions

1. How do I treat my "home" – my body?

2. What habits are depleting my physical and mental energy, and how can I change them?

3. When does my body feel its best, and how can I recreate those conditions daily?

Closing Words – Listening to the Body

The body isn't just the servant of the mind; it's also its teacher. By nurturing it through nutrition, movement, rest, and healthy routines, we build a strong foundation for our life's journey.

Listening to the body allows us to connect with our inner energy and achieve balance that translates into both strength and well-being—from the inside out.

Answer the questions and meditate for 10 minutes. Reflect on what you are sensing after this work and write it down

Day 21

The Being – The Journey of Inner Growth and Self-Discovery

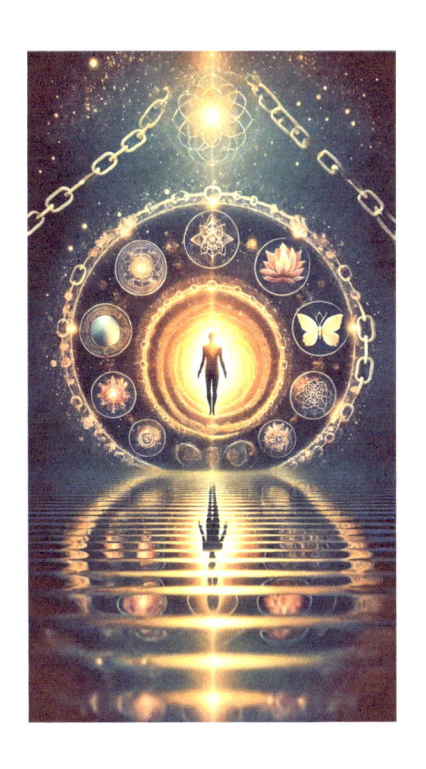

Chapter 21 takes us on another exciting journey. Discovering and nurturing your inner being is a journey of awareness, transformation, and mindful living. Through self-reflection, courage, and intentional habits, you can break free from old patterns and live a life that reflects your true self.

Take a deep breath and meditate for 5 minutes

The Journey of Inner Growth and Self-Discovery

"Your being is like a tree in an ever-changing forest; with strong roots of self-awareness, it can weather storms, shed old leaves, and grow anew toward the light of purpose and possibility."

In day 6, "Building a new personality", I delve into how becoming more self-aware, confronting my inner struggles, and embracing new experiences can help me transform old patterns, cultivate inner prosperity, and bring harmony to both my mind and body.

In day 11, "The journey", I see life as a transformative journey of growth, learning, and evolution. By letting go of resistance, embracing change, and nurturing my self-awareness, I move toward balance, peace, and meaningful progress.

. . .

In day 16, "Understanding the world better", I emphasize the transformative power of reading and building meaningful connections. By prioritizing these over modern distractions, I cultivate self-awareness, nurture my emotional well-being, and strengthen genuine relationships through reflective practices.

> *"Joy in life is nature's test of a perfect existence. When a person is happy, they are true to themselves and living in harmony with life."*
> – Oscar Wilde

Life is a journey full of challenges, opportunities, and endless lessons. Our character—what distinguishes us from others—is constantly shaped by our behavior, habits, and thoughts.

This journey requires awareness, resilience, and the courage to face oneself.

> As Johann Wolfgang von Goethe observed: *"Man can endure anything except for one dull day after another."*

By cultivating self-awareness and working diligently on healthy lifestyle habits, we can transform old patterns and create a life that reflects our inner strength, values, and purpose.

> As Icelandic theologian Karl Sigurbjörnsson put it: *"A good life is not about having it easy but about doing good for others."*

Life mirrors what we invest in it. Awareness of what consciously and unconsciously drives us allows us to choose our path forward.

> Voltaire reminds us: *"Without care, the soul easily becomes a trash bin that we endlessly postpone cleaning."*

When we nurture ourselves both inside and out, we have the

potential to turn life's journey into a rich experience, fostering balance, peace, and purpose.

Each decision, no matter how small, can be a step toward a more fulfilling and joyful life.

Transformative elements

Risk-Taking and Connection or Fear and Withdrawal
Transformation begins with risk-taking. It takes courage to let go of the old and open up to new opportunities.

Connecting deeply with others and ourselves requires mindfulness and intention.

René Magritte's words resonate here: *"Everything visible hides something invisible."*

Key Steps:

Awareness Creates Choice

Being mindful of your thoughts, habits, and relationships opens the door to change.

Understanding Yourself and Your Past

We often carry unconscious patterns from childhood that hold us back.

Examining and understanding these patterns enables us to make intentional changes.

Progress Over Perfection
Growth doesn't happen in leaps but in steady steps forward. As the saying goes: *"Dripping water hollows out the stone."*

. . .

How to Begin

1. *Get the Ball Rolling*
   - Small successes lead to bigger ones. Once you see results, it becomes easier to continue.
2. *Reassess Your Toolbox*
   - You can't build a new life with old tools. Identify what no longer serves you and find new solutions.
3. *Activate Your Inner Strength*
   - Practices like meditation and self-reflection unlock new perspectives and possibilities.
4. *Take Responsibility*
   - Happiness is the sum of small, value-based decisions made consistently.

Spiritual Preparation – The Key to Growth
"The fundamental human need is growth. We strive to find a place where preparation meets opportunity."

Focus Areas:

1. *Listen to Your Heart*
   - Disconnecting from your heart disconnects you from your inner power. Reclaim this connection by attending to your needs and desires.
2. *Recognize Barriers*
   - What is holding you back? What can you release to open new doors?
3. *Let Go of the Past*
   - Growth requires releasing what no longer serves you.

———

Søren Kierkegaard aptly observed:
"Life is not a problem to be solved, but a reality to be experienced."

"If you have the courage to say goodbye to what no longer serves you, life will reward you with new opportunities."

Cultivating your being – Practical Steps
"If you have a strong purpose in life, you don't have to be pushed. Your passion will drive you there."

1. *Self-Reflection*
   - Ask yourself: What within me am I grateful for?
   - What are my strengths, and how can I use them more effectively?
2. *Reframing Habits*
   - *Foundations:* What habits shape your day?
   - *Patterns:* What routines have you created, and how do they impact your life?
3. *Energy Pie Exercise*
   - Map out how you use your energy:
     - What gives you energy?
     - What drains it?
   - This exercise helps prioritize what matters and achieve balance.
4. *Release the Past*
   - While you may not have chosen your childhood circumstances, you now have the power to decide how you respond. Awareness is the key to freedom from unconscious patterns.

Reflections on the Past and Mindfulness
"You can take a person out of a situation, but removing the situation from the person is the greater challenge."

We often repeat old patterns, even when we know they no longer serve us. By viewing these patterns with openness and understanding, we can free ourselves to change.

Working with the Subconscious
Steps to Address Patterns:

1. *Identify the Patterns*
   - Are current circumstances tied to unconscious patterns from the past?
2. *Awareness and Action*
   - Recognizing these patterns and consciously addressing them unlocks new possibilities.

The Power of Thoughts
Our thoughts shape our emotions, behaviors, and destiny. Allowing fear or doubt to dominate creates tension that keeps us from living fully in the present.

- *Be mindful of your thoughts—they become words.*

- *Be mindful of your words—they become actions.*

- *Be mindful of your actions—they become habits.*

- *Be mindful of your habits—they become your character.*

- *Be mindful of your character—it becomes your destiny.*

A Real-Life Story – Small changes lead to Transformation

Josephine had always felt stuck in relationships where she was disrespected.

She realized this pattern stemmed from her childhood—seeking to please everyone to avoid conflict. Her subconscious had programmed her to tolerate harmful situations.

With increased awareness, Josephine began taking small, empowering steps. She learned to respect her own boundaries, say "no" when necessary, and surround herself with people who brought her joy and safety. These small changes transformed her life, giving her the freedom to create healthier patterns.

What Life Teaches – Emotions as Behavior Seeking Balance

We often forgive those who speak ill of us, yet we struggle to forgive those about whom we speak ill.

Our emotional state often reflects thoughts and memories connected to the present moment. If these thoughts are colored by unresolved emotions, life becomes more complicated.

However, by recognizing this, we can break old patterns and create a new sense of balance.

Understanding that emotions are a guide rather than a burden allows us to approach life with greater clarity and peace. Balance arises when we acknowledge and address the roots of our feelings, paving the way for personal growth and harmony.

Self-Reflecting Questions

1. What do I need to let go of to make space for something new in my life?

2. Who in my environment provides the support and peace I need on this journey?

3. How can I balance challenges and skills to nurture my inner drive?

Closing Words – Becoming the Master of Your Life

Your being isn't just a state—it's a process. It's a journey of self-discovery, habit transformation, and balance. With mindfulness and self-reflection, you can create a life that reflects your best self.

"Flow is freedom! "Step out of old patterns and let new possibilities flourish. *Take care of the present—soon it will be the past.*

Answer the questions and meditate for 10 minutes. Reflect on what you are sensing after this work and write it down

Day 22

The Cost of Inaction – Breaking Free from Limiting Patterns

T his chapter emphasizes the high price of avoiding responsibility and delaying action in areas like health, relationships, and self-growth, while offering strategies for creating change through awareness, accountability, and small, consistent steps.

Take a deep breath and meditate for 5 minutes

Breaking Free from Limiting Patterns

"Inaction is like a leaking roof during a storm—each drop seems insignificant at first, but over time, the water erodes the foundation, leaving you with a much greater problem to repair. Taking action is the act of fixing the leak before the damage grows beyond control."

In day 7, "The 5% syndrome", I dive into the concept of my internal "operating system," uncovering how outdated habits and recurring thought patterns consume 95% of my mental energy. By taking actionable steps, I learn to redesign this system, creating a more conscious, balanced, and fulfilling life.

In day 12, "Are you free or a prisoner", I reflect on my journey from self-imposed emotional imprisonment—shaped by past traumas and fear of others' opinions—to the freedom I've found through self-acceptance, forgiveness, and living in alignment with my own values.

. . .

In day 17, "The judge", I delve into the pervasive presence of my inner judge, exploring how it shapes my life. Through tools and reflections, I learn to transform harsh self-criticism and judgment into compassion, self-awareness, and understanding, fostering deeper connections with both myself and others.

The Price of Inaction

Communication mirrors our self-respect and accountability. When we fail to set clear boundaries or accept disrespect, we unknowingly establish a pattern where such behavior becomes normalized. Our subconscious, like Pavlov's dogs reacting to a bell, directs us back to familiar experiences of mistreatment, albeit in different forms.

Each time we allow ourselves to be mistreated, we silently grant permission for it to continue. Learning to stand up for ourselves might cause discomfort in the moment, but it prevents deeper pain and the erosion of our self-worth over time.

MY STORY

I had a dream of belonging to a family—a dream I had never experienced but deeply longed for. I also dreamt of owning my own apartment, something that felt distant and unattainable. These aspirations shaped my early life and gave me hope.

The Dream of a Family

At 22, I met my wife. She was like an angel in my life—warm and kind, even when I faltered and made mistakes. Despite everything, she remained my partner. Our relationship was a precious mirror, reflecting my weaknesses and the inner work I needed to do.

. . .

The Apartment - A Space of My Own

At 25, I bought a brand-new apartment. It wasn't just a place to live; it was a home equipped with everything I needed. Moving into a newly built home felt like a victory—a dream realized and a symbol of freedom.

My Daughter - The Light of My Life

That same year, I became a father to a healthy baby girl. She has been the greatest gift of my life, loving me unconditionally. She is a constant reminder that love, and connection give life meaning.

The Patterns That Held Me Back

Despite these blessings—family, home, and love—I remained trapped in patterns learned during childhood. I had spent my life practicing detachment and avoidance.

These internal struggles led me to abandon situations I didn't know how to handle. I moved into an old, dreary basement apartment, which felt like a relief at the time.

But it also revealed a self-perception as an "unworthy bargain item," undeserving of happiness. I realized that unresolved wounds—whether created by circumstances or myself—come at a cost.

These unhealed patterns continued to control my life, even though I had everything I once dreamed of.

Key Takeaways:

1. *Self-Perception Shapes Decisions*: Even when I achieved my dreams, old patterns and unresolved wounds influenced how I received and valued them.

2. *Acknowledging Roots:* My childhood and life circumstances had roots that needed acknowledgment. By confronting these roots, I could begin taking responsibility for their impact on my life.
3. *Real Change from Within***:** Escaping or changing environments is only a temporary solution. Lasting change requires internal work and balance.

Transformative elements

The Cost of Ignoring What Needs to Be Done:
Every day offers choices that impact our physical and mental well-being. When we avoid taking responsibility for what we know is good for us, it accumulates into discomfort and imbalance. The price of inaction is higher than we often realize—it affects our relationships, health, and self-image.

Daily Choices: The Foundation of Well-Being
Small, postponed decisions—like exercising, eating well, or addressing communication issues—have ripple effects on our lives:

- *Relationships:* Overstepping boundaries without apologizing creates discomfort and tension.
- *Physical Health:* Prolonged sitting or skipping stretches harms our body and mind.
- *Nutrition:* Poor dietary choices lead to fatigue, irritability, and imbalance.
- *Family and Friends:* Neglecting relationships causes bonds to fade over time.

What Happens When We Delay Action?
Unaddressed issues manifest as discomfort, stress, and even health problems.

1. *Signals from the Body:* Neglecting exercise or proper nutrition results in pain, fatigue, and irritation.
2. *Communication:* Failing to assert boundaries fosters inner turmoil, making disrespect from others the norm.
3. *Mental Well-Being:* Neglecting self-care leads to loneliness and anxiety.

A Real-Life Story

A close friend once said, "I'll just finish one more deal." He could feel his nervous system breaking down but pushed through.

The deal took longer than expected, and his stubbornness prevented him from resting. Suddenly, he suffered a stroke and never fully recovered.

This story illustrates how ignoring warning signs from our body and life can lead to devastating consequences.

Learning from Delayed Action

Life always shows us the consequences of procrastination or neglect. While these effects may not be immediate, they eventually surface as dissatisfaction or imbalance.

- *Communication*

Allowing others to mistreat us without addressing it leads to accumulated disrespect.

- *Health*

Regular exercise, nutrition, and routines are gifts to our future selves. Neglecting them costs us later.

- *Connections*

Prioritizing our own needs over relationships results in isolation and weakened bonds.

The Cost of Failing to Break Patterns

Without addressing limiting patterns, we remain stuck in cycles of dissatisfaction.

- *Impatience Breeds Stress*

Letting impatience take over disrupts peace and flow.

- *Poor Health*

Neglecting our bodies leads to discomfort and illness.

- *Damaged Relationships*

Failing to nurture family and friendships creates distance and fear of loss.

Solutions - Small Steps That Make a Difference

1. *Awareness*

Ask yourself, "What is the cost of not doing this?" Understanding consequences motivates change.

2. *Daily Habits*

Simple practices like exercising, meditating, or reaching out to loved ones can transform health and well-being.

3. *Accountability*

Stand up for yourself in communication. Speak your truth clearly and assertively.

4. *Connect with Your Body*

Listen to its signals and respond with action, not excuses.

A Practical Example:
When feeling stressed in a conversation, take a walk or listen to calming music. Give yourself "me-time" to reset before addressing the issue.

Self-Reflecting Questions

1. What have you been delaying that could improve your well-being?
2. What are the consequences of not addressing it?
3. How can you introduce a small habit today to steer yourself in the right direction?

Final Words - The Cost Is the Cost

What we do today lays the foundation for who we become tomorrow.

Taking responsibility for small, daily decisions strengthens us for the future.

Ignoring our needs always comes back to us—sometimes in harm that's hard to undo.

By listening to our bodies, nurturing relationships, and creating healthy habits, we can transform our lives and find lasting balance.

Answer the questions and meditate for 10 minutes. Reflect on what you are sensing after this work and write it down

Day 23
To Love and Be Loved

In this chapter we explore the transformative power of love, emphasizing vulnerability, trust, and understanding as essential elements for building meaningful relationships and fostering intimacy.

Take a deep breath and meditate for 5 minutes

To Love and Be Loved

"Love is like tending a garden—it thrives when nurtured with care, attention, and trust. Just as plants need sunlight, water, and fertile soil, relationships flourish with warmth, understanding, and vulnerability. Neglecting the garden allows weeds of fear and misunderstanding to grow, but consistent effort reveals the beauty and strength hidden within."

In day 8, "Communication", I explore how practicing mindful communication—grounded in respect, understanding, and self-awareness—helps me foster stronger connections, support emotional growth, and cultivate inner peace.

By focusing on building bridges instead of walls, I nurture healthier and more meaningful relationships.

In day 13, "Embracing what is", I explore the importance of appreciating the present, releasing old patterns, and nurturing love and respect in my relationships. These are the keys to finding inner peace and experiencing true happiness.

. . .

In day 18, "Active with yourself", I explore my journey from co-dependence to self-respect is one of transformation through self-awareness, boundary-setting, and embracing my authentic self. By making conscious decisions and reflecting deeply, I learn to balance supporting others while preserving my own peace and integrity.

To Love and Be Loved

Love is both a force and a mystery—a vital energy that connects us to deeper purpose and well-being.

> As Guðmundur Ingólfsson and Magnús Haraldsson put it: "Love is like a bushfire, Love is a magnet, from a small spark, a great blaze often ignites. Love is like white magic; it fills body and soul."

Love is not a commonplace, but it is essential. A healthy romantic relationship, built on mutual trust and warmth, deeply influences our energy levels and quality of life.

Love helps us release the past, forgive, and cultivate peace and happiness. The most powerful addiction under the sun is the longing to love and to be loved, and life can flourish when we have a loving connection with another person.

Relationships are not perfect. Hiding emotions or discontent can damage trust. However, flaws are often forgivable when they are laid out with honesty and care.

Opening the Gate and Bridging the Gap

Not everyone has positive role models for building healthy romantic relationships. This can lead to fear of rejection or uncertainty about how to express oneself. How do we learn to share our hearts in a healthy way, despite our fears?

. . .

Imagine a shared bowl of the heart—where two individuals pour out their innermost truths. If we encounter resistance when we are vulnerable, it can harm trust. The solution lies in agreeing that attacking someone who opens their heart is not acceptable.

Love is both a force and a mystery. It heals, connects, and strengthens. As stated in 1 Corinthians 13:

"*Love covers a multitude of sins.*" When we show others love and tolerance, we receive the same in return, and the relationship grows stronger. When we give our best, we earn the highest quality of patience and grace from our partner.

Transformative elements

Connection and Intimacy

The strongest craving under the sun is the desire to be loved. Intimacy is built on the ability to share our innermost truths without fear of rejection. Hearing "You are safe with me" deepens the connection.

"The 5 Love Languages by Gary Chapman" – Ways to Nurture Love:

1. *Words of Affirmation*
   - Encouragement, kind words, and validation strengthen trust.
   - Messages that show appreciation and understanding for your partner are key.
2. *Quality Time*
   - Give undivided attention and acceptance.
   - Genuine presence fosters deeper connections.
3. *Acts of Service*
   - Small, loving gestures can have a big impact.
   - Simple examples: bringing coffee to bed or taking the car to the mechanic.

4. *Gifts*
    - Personal and meaningful gifts demonstrate attentiveness and interest.
5. *Physical Touch*
    - Kisses, cuddling, and intimacy are ways to show and feel love and security.

Hiding is Stealing

Love is a complex phenomenon, often illogical and transcending boundaries.

We suppress our feelings because of pain we don't understand, but when we learn to confront it, we can find deep peace and build healthy connections.

Research on Happiness

Harvard University has been studying what makes people happy since 1934. The main findings highlight the importance of relationships.

- Healthy relationships strengthen our inner foundations and make us whole individuals.
- Trust is the foundation of close relationships. When we allow ourselves to be who we truly are, we create peace and security from within.
- Belonging gives life deeper meaning and calms the mind.

Facing Rejection and Building Connections

The fear of not being enough or of rejection can fuel anxiety and depression.

The solution is to take the risk and be vulnerable.

Sharing your heart with another person without fear of rejection can nurture the relationship.

This requires:

- *Setting boundaries*

These illuminate your mental and emotional state as well as others'. Responses often reveal more than words.

- *Practicing active listening*

Listen not to reply, but to understand.

- *Choosing words carefully*

Statements like "When you say/do this, I feel…" provide space for understanding your feelings.

Flaws and Relationship Guidelines

No relationship is perfect. Flaws, however, can be forgiven if approached with love and understanding.
Relationship Traffic Rules:

- Show warmth and admiration toward each other.
- Be willing to apologize when things go awry.

Examples:

- "Love, are you running a red light right now?"

- "I'm sorry, my heart. I've had a tough day, but you shouldn't have to bear the brunt of it. Hug!"

These examples shows how flaws can be met with empathy and care, strengthening rather than harming the relationship.

. . .

Love and Health

Love is more than a feeling—it is a choice we make every day.

By showing warmth, understanding, and affection, we receive energy, joy, and balance in return.

A Real-Life Story - The Gateway of the Heart

Isak was always afraid to be open in his relationships. He had often felt rejected and insecure when trying to share his emotions.

When he met Jane, he decided to open up gradually. He told her about his fear of rejection. Jane responded: *"You are safe with me. I will not judge you."*

These words became a turning point for Isak—they built trust and intimacy between them.

Over time, they both learned to share their innermost truths without fear, and their relationship flourished.

Self-Reflecting Questions

1. How can you deepen intimacy in your relationships by sharing your innermost truths and providing safety and support?
2. What is your partner's (or loved one's) love language, and how can you use it to strengthen your bond?
3. How do you handle flaws in relationships? What steps can you take to approach difficult situations with warmth and understanding?

Final Words

Love is a life force that builds us up. By opening our hearts, providing others with security, and creating space for truth, we gain healthier and stronger connections.

Answer the questions and meditate for 10 minutes. Reflect on what you are sensing after this work and write it down

Day 24

Addiction – Understanding Its Roots and Transforming Its Drive

This chapter delves into the roots of addiction, framing it as a developmental response to unaddressed pain, and offers strategies to break free through self-awareness, discipline, and the transformation of unhealthy impulses into positive energy, leading to authentic freedom and connection.

Take a deep breath and meditate for 5 minutes

Metaphor for Addiction – Understanding Its Roots and Transforming Its Drive

"Addiction is like a tree with tangled roots growing in the shadow of pain. The more it is fed, the deeper its roots dig into the soil, entwining our sense of freedom. Breaking free requires cutting away the overgrowth, tracing its roots to their source, and planting seeds of self-awareness and discipline that can grow into a forest of strength and renewal."

"A suspicion crept upon me that something inside me had died at the well of the house. People also have load-bearing beams, and they, too, can fall."
– Jón Kalman

Addiction as a Process and Response

Addiction is not a simple behavior but a developmental process—a way to seek and manage happiness.

It can be likened to cancer, with cells multiplying uncontrollably. In its early stages, addiction often serves as a method to numb pain or discomfort we cannot explain.

It enslaves us to that which defeats us and becomes our shortcut to temporary relief, even when it results in long-term suffering.

My Story

In 1996, my friend Gulli said to me, shortly after I had completed rehab: "The only things I want are the things that are bad for me." I thought, *Wow, he's really unwell.* It took me 20 years to understand the depth of what Gulli had said. It's the root that sustains the branches, not the branches that sustain the root.

In 2019, I went to see a psychologist. My brother recommended him, saying he was an exceptionally skilled and compassionate person. Todd asked me what I wanted to achieve from our work together. I said, "I want to change the root—from being an addict to becoming a life coach."

My upbringing shaped this journey: My father was a severely ill alcoholic and gambling addict. My mother had endured a difficult childhood, struggled with co-dependency, and eventually turned to drinking. As a highly sensitive child, I suffered greatly.

I was burdened with deep feelings of inferiority and overwhelming fear. I was terrified that others would find out how terrible I truly was and reject me. I became a people-pleaser, doing everything I could to gain approval.

This fear created a dark voice inside me, a voice that spoke in my weakest moments, amplifying my anxiety and making me feel even smaller.

. . .

My addictions began to take hold

- *Daydreaming* - My first addiction was escaping into a fantasy world where everything was perfect.

- *Food* - I turned to food for comfort, using it to alter my mood.

1. Slot Machines

Slot machines were my first real love. I lived for them. Though they were off-limits to anyone under 16, I started playing as much as I could at age 11.

Jói, the owner of a convenience store with slot machines, became my worst enemy. He refused to give me the coins I needed to play, claiming he didn't have change.

It took me years to realize he was trying to protect me.

Soon, my friends and I started playing billiards and poker for money.

I quickly became very skilled at billiards and decent at poker, which often left me flush with cash.

I've since learned that the high from gambling is chemically similar to the effects of cocaine.

I was constantly in a high state, even grinding my teeth in my sleep at a young age.

2. Nicotine

Too scared to start smoking, I turned to snuff and later General tobacco pouches.

. . .

3. Pornography has been my worst addiction

It ignited the spark of my attachment disorder, which has been my greatest disability.

4. Alcohol

Having witnessed the damage caused by alcohol, I vowed never to drink. But a person out of balance is like a house divided against itself.

At 14, I began drinking, and for the first time, I felt free. I could talk to girls and express myself.

For eight years, I was drunk at every opportunity. A year before I quit drinking, I started using drugs. This rapidly accelerated my downfall.

At 22, I hit rock bottom and entered rehab. I still remember the relief of being in treatment. Not being hungover every weekend felt like a revelation.

Transformative elements

Why Do We Numb Ourselves?

> *"Many a traveller sets out with a broken heart, for them, the world needs people willing to offer a pat on the back.*
>
> *Without that support, they keep driving year after year in deep despair, becoming self-made grinding machines others try to fix."*
>
> – GG

We numb ourselves due to pain we don't understand, shame we've internalized, or a false self we've built.

This false self amplifies our flaws, condemns us for our mistakes, and makes us inconsistent with our true selves. This cycle perpetuates imbalance—imbalance that calls for more imbalance.

Temptations and Self-Discipline

Temptations often arrive like beggars entering through doors we ourselves have left open. They grow in strength when indulged and expand their reach over time.

Self-respect is built on self-discipline; denying harmful temptations is the foundation of our sense of worth.

The Path to Self-Integrity and Healing

> *"Maybe you are searching among the branches for what appears in the roots."*
> – Rumi

To understand addiction and transform it, we must look inward and ask ourselves:

- How can I build a relationship with myself and grow closer to my authentic being?
- What methods do I use to achieve short-term relief that cause long-term discomfort?
- How can I turn lower impulses into positive driving forces?

Numbing and the Journey Through Life

When we numb ourselves, whether through addiction or other means, it is akin to urinating in a shoe in the frost—it feels warm at first but soon freezes, leaving behind an unpleasant Odor.

This metaphor captures how we get stuck in unhealthy patterns, allowing addiction to dominate our lives.

True freedom lies in maintaining control over all we do—being mindful and making informed choices.

Reflections on Hope, Simplicity, and Courage
Life is a journey, with hope serving as a guiding light in the darkness.

> William F. Lynch noted: *"One of hope's best anchors is to find areas of despair and face them—not with desperation, but with the intention of not allowing them to taint the realms of possibility."*

By acknowledging the parts of life that fill us with fear or doubt, we can turn them into opportunities for growth and change.

> James Allen emphasized the power of conscious thought: *"The best weapon against stress is the ability to choose one thought over another."*

When we commit to simplifying life, shedding the unnecessary, and focusing on what truly matters, we create space for clarity and inner peace. *"No one is blinder than the one who refuses to see."*

These words remind us to open our eyes to our own truths and take responsibility for what we can change. Often, the burden we choose to bear alone is the heaviest, but acknowledging the need for help and connection is where true strength lies.

Inspiration for Transformation

> *"The truth you hesitate to accept is the foundation of your liberation."*
> – Joseph Campbell

"If you tell the truth, it becomes a part of your past. But if you lie, it becomes a part of your future."

William Faulkner observed: *"You cannot swim for new horizons until you have courage to lose sight of the shore."*

Letting go of the old takes courage, but only through such surrender can we discover the opportunities and possibilities beyond our current horizons.

Key Principles for Change and Hope:

1. *Acknowledgment:* Facing difficulties without despair.
2. *Conscious Thought:* Choosing thoughts that bring us closer to the life we desire.
3. *Simplicity:* Clearing away the clutter in our minds and lives, allowing hope and purpose to thrive.
4. *Courage:* Stepping into the unknown, even when we can't see the entire path ahead.

Inner World, Flaws, and Connections
What story do I use to justify my flaws? We often craft narratives to explain our behaviors or shortcomings. For example: *"He never listens to me, so I..."*

These stories often serve as defense mechanisms to avoid facing our own responsibility or pain. They shape our relationships—both with ourselves and others. *"The relationship you have with yourself reflects your inner world."*

If your inner world is filled with self-criticism, fear, or insecurity, this will be mirrored in your interactions. If you find peace and self-respect within, you can create better connections with others.

Mother Teresa once said: *"It is not hunger but loneliness that plagues this world."*

Despite the technological revolution that has increased connectivity through devices and social media, loneliness has grown.

This makes it clearer than ever that the relationship we have with ourselves is the foundation of our connections with others.

The Three-Headed Beast – Forces That Keep Us Stuck:

1. *Need* - Constantly trying to fill an inner void can lead to dependence on things that provide temporary comfort but long-term harm.

2. *Abstinence* - Understanding what we need to distance ourselves from and why.

- *What excites you?*
  - *What makes you absent in your own life?*

3. *The Body Craves What It Contains* - Habits and lifestyles create demands we often fulfill unconsciously.

Pain That Brings Resolution – What Is It?

It might be the pain of letting go of what harms us or confronting a difficult truth. When the present pain outweighs the past, it can become a catalyst for change.

"Reality can be hell when you're just visiting." Avoiding reality leaves us in discord and imbalance. Dwelling in reality requires courage and a willingness to change.

Breaking the Cycle of Addiction

We often return to familiar situations, even when they are harmful. To break free, we must:

- Map out the patterns that keep us stuck.
- Understand how the three-headed beast—need, abstinence, and physical cravings—controls us.
- Face the pain with a willingness to create solutions.

Inspirational Quotes

1. "What comes around goes around if you stick around." – What you tolerate persists. Breaking free from unhealthy patterns requires stepping away.

2. "We don't rise to the level of expectations; we fall to the level of our training." – Lasting change comes from consistent self-work and practice.

3. "The courage to leave behind what no longer serves you is the same courage that will guide you to what does."

Self-Reflecting Questions

1. What methods do I use to avoid pain, and how do they affect my life?
2. How can self-discipline help me reclaim self-respect and control?
3. What lower impulses could I transform into positive motivation?

Final Words - Temptation that is indulged grows stronger

Temptations often enter through doors we intentionally open. Temptation is like a beggar—if treated kindly, it returns with friends.

Are we living for fleeting fixes or meaningful experiences?

True freedom lies in having nothing to hide and embracing life with authenticity.

Answer the questions and meditate for 10 minutes. Reflect on what you are sensing after this work and write it down

Day 25
Work – The Process and the Rewards

Chapter 25 emphasizes that work is not just about completing tasks but about personal growth, fostering positive relationships, and creating opportunities through ambition, responsibility, and a proactive attitude.

Take a deep breath and meditate for 5 minutes

The Process and the Rewards

"Work is like a garden—what you plant and nurture grows, whether it's weeds of complaint or flowers of effort and ambition.

By cultivating the soil of relationships, watering with diligence, and pruning negativity, you transform the workplace into a thriving ecosystem that not only rewards you but also reflects who you are becoming."

Work – The Process and the Rewards

"The highest reward for a person's toil is not what they get for it, but what they become by it."
– John Ruskin

Working well is not just about completing tasks or earning a paycheck; it is a process that fosters growth, personal development, and opportunities.

Staying focused is a vital skill, and the key is to concentrate on one task at a time, complete it, and disconnect when the workday ends.

If you find your job boring or dread Mondays, it may be time to consider new opportunities.

Research shows that most heart attacks happen on Monday mornings, emphasizing the importance of finding work that brings purpose to your life.

Studies also indicate that four out of five people go to work focused more on serving their own needs than their employer's. This highlights the need for balance between personal needs and workplace responsibilities.

What you give is what you receive. If you feel something is missing, ask yourself whether you are giving it. Each day is a chance to lay the foundation for the future, and how you approach your work affects both your career and well-being.

My story

In 2018, I started a new job and set a goal to become the best employee in the company. I went above and beyond, not just with my tasks but also by participating in projects outside my direct responsibilities. This goal became my guiding principle at work and influenced how I felt.

I found joy and pride in doing things well. Praise from my employer and colleagues confirmed I was on the right path.

When I eventually resigned, my employer was disappointed, but I knew I had given my best with integrity and professionalism.

What motivated me to leave was the desire to write this book —a dream that demanded my full attention and time. 😊

Transformative elements

Ways to Excel at Work:

1. *Show Ambition and Responsibility*
    - Be faithful in small things; this builds trust and leads to greater opportunities.
    - Think of your paycheck as a sign that you are a valuable investment for your employer.
    - Arrive on time, preferably a little early, and don't rush to leave.

2. *Go Above and Beyond*
    - Strive to show up as your best self—both physically and mentally.
    - Take tasks a step further and find ways to improve your environment.

3. *Build Relationships and Good Karma*
    - You reap what you sow. Life will repay you in kind.
    - Create positive energy in your workplace through warmth and camaraderie.

Simple Ways to Improve Your Work and Environment:

1. *Connecting with People*
    - Smile with your eyes and greet people by name.
    - Talk *to* people, not *about* them.
    - Offer praise and support—positive energy creates a better work environment.

2. *Respecting the Environment*
    - See trash? Pick it up.
    - Notice something that could be improved? Offer solutions, not complaints.
    - Speak positively about your employer—they pay your bills.

3. *Conduct and Behavior*
    - Be neat in appearance and diligent in your work.
    - Be the head, not the tail—take initiative.
    - If your intuition tells you to talk to your manager, don't hesitate.

Self-Control and Success
Research shows that people with good self-control:

- Maintain better relationships.

- Demonstrate more empathy and emotional balance.

- Are less susceptible to depression and mood swings.

Healthy workplaces promote well-being by:

- Encouraging physical activity with access to fitness facilities.

- Organizing healthy, alcohol-free social events.

A Real-Life Story – Changing Your Attitude Toward Work

Maria was diligent in her job but often felt undervalued. She frequently complained to her colleagues about how her employer failed to appreciate her contributions.

One day, she realized that these negative thoughts were dragging her down and affecting her well-being.

Instead of waiting for recognition from others, she decided to change her approach.

She began taking more initiative, sharing new ideas, and praising her colleagues.

Within a few months, her employer noticed the change and gave her more responsibilities.

Maria experienced increased motivation, well-being, and even joy in her work.

Self-Reflecting Questions

1. How can I show more ambition and initiative in my work?

2. How can I contribute to a better work environment for myself and others?

3. What small change could have the most significant impact on my job performance and well-being?

Final Words

Those who focus on doing their job well, rather than just getting paid, will excel—both in their career and in life.

"Do what you can today with passion and responsibility. Life will reward you with opportunities you.

Answer the questions and meditate for 10 minutes. Reflect on what you are sensing after this work and write it down

Day 26

The Toolbox for a Better Life –
Cultivating Lifestyle Through Conscious Habits and Tools

This chapter provides practical tools and strategies to establish healthy habits, overcome inner obstacles, and build a balanced lifestyle, emphasizing the importance of reflection, intentional living, and gradual, positive changes.

Take a deep breath and meditate for 5 minutes

Cultivating Lifestyle Through Conscious Habits and Tools:
"Life is like building a house: your habits are the tools, your values are the blueprint, and each small, intentional action lays another brick in the foundation of a balanced, fulfilling life.

Just as a sturdy home requires regular maintenance and careful craftsmanship, a meaningful life depends on consistent reflection, effort, and the willingness to refine what isn't working."

To live a meaningful and conscious life, we must use tools that enhance mental and physical strength.

These are simple methods that help create balance and well-being in daily life. By adopting healthy habits, we cultivate inner positivity, reduce stress, and build a lifestyle that aligns with our goals.

Tools for a Better Life:
Re-evaluation - To keep your mind clear and goals aligned:

- Take time once a week to review your "top ten list" in writing.

- Adjust your compass by letting go of what isn't working and assessing what needs improvement.

- Discuss emotional challenges with someone you trust to foster brain growth.

Healthy Fats - Your brain thrives on nourishment from healthy fats:

- Examples - Avocado oil, hemp oil, flaxseed oil.

- Take one tablespoon per 25 kg of body weight daily.

- These oils reduce cravings for sweets, nourish the brain, and promote overall health.

Rest

- Meditation acts as a "time-out" for the brain.

- It boosts intelligence, enhances focus, and helps you be more present.

Exercise - Movement significantly improves health, especially brain health:

- Increases happiness and improves sleep.

- Helps lower blood pressure and enhances oxygen intake.

- Strengthens muscles, bones, and joints.

- Expands heart chambers and boosts their capacity.

- Regular exercise can lower your resting heart rate by 10 beats in 10 weeks.

Set a Goal and Write Down 5 Reasons Why the Current Situation is Unacceptable:

1. *Clarity* - Identifying why your current state isn't satisfactory helps motivate change.
2. *Accountability* - Writing reasons strengthens your commitment to the goal.
3. *Perspective* - It highlights the gaps between where you are and where you want to be.
4. *Motivation* - Understanding the discomfort of staying the same fuels your drive to act.
5. *Direction* - It provides a clear starting point to begin moving toward improvement.

My Story - Morning Pages, why Are They So Powerful?

"The Artist's Way Morning Pages Journal"
— Julia Cameron

I've written morning pages for 10 years, and they are one of the greatest gifts in my life. They bring clarity and nurture my creativity.

Morning pages are a daily tool for connecting with yourself. More than writing, they are a spiritual process that can transform how you think, create, and approach life.

By jotting down your thoughts freely, without judgment or

expectations, you open doors to inner awareness and creativity. *Benefits of Morning Pages:*

1. *Reduce Self-Doubt*
   - Writing allows surface thoughts like fear of inadequacy or self-doubt to flow freely. Over time, their power diminishes.
   - *How?* You train yourself to see your thoughts as they are—just thoughts, not truths.

2. *Quiet the Inner Critic*
   - Morning pages act as a practice to silence the inner voice that diminishes you. Writing without concern for quality or purpose creates an unrestricted space.
   - *Impact:* You let go of perfectionism and feel freer to create without fear of judgment.

3. *Increase Awareness*
   - Morning pages function like mental windshield wipers, clearing cloudy thoughts and offering clearer insight into your inner world.
   - *Example:* You might discover self-sabotaging behavior or unrecognized desires.

4. *Reconnect with Creativity*
   - Creativity isn't just for artists; it's a life force within us all. Morning pages tap into this energy, uncovering new ideas, solutions, and possibilities.
   - *Impact:* They liberate self-expression and reveal your unique talents and intuition.

5. *Clarify Dreams and Desires*
   - Writing regularly makes it easier to discern what

you truly want. Morning pages help you align with your values and pursue your goals.
- *Example:* You might realize certain goals or relationships don't align with your values.

6. *Build Support Networks*
    - Morning pages teach you how to support yourself and recognize who truly uplifts you. Writing increases awareness of strengthening and draining relationships.

Master-Level Benefits:

- Break down negative beliefs that hinder you.
- Highlight obstacles on your path.
- Celebrate and pursue your dreams.
- Teach you how to nurture yourself and build meaningful connections.

Transformative elements

Nicknames for Inner Obstacles

Inspired by Julia Cameron's *The Artist's Way,* naming your internal challenges helps you understand and work with them rather than be controlled by them. *Examples:*

1. *The Heart's Foolish Warrior*
    - *Traits* - Chases novelty and excitement, leaving safe and warm spaces for the unknown.
    - *Behavior* - Constantly seeks new emotions or passions when the current one fades.
    - *Impact* - Frequent changes prevent deep connections with oneself and others.

2. *Bobby the Imbalance Master*

- *Traits* - Spends half the time out of balance—emotionally, physically, or mentally.
- *Behavior* - Over-trains, binge eats and gets stuck in cycles of weight gain and loss of self-respect.
- *Impact* - Develops insecurity and struggles to break patterns.

3. *Lucky Larry*
    - *Traits* - Tends to uproot himself, rejecting the good in life.
    - *Behavior* - Leaves loving partners, moves frequently, and ends up empty-handed.
    - *Impact* - Deepens heartbreak with each departure, leaving lasting scars.

4. *The Addict Master*
    - *Traits* - Keeps you locked in patterns of impulsivity and short-term gratification.
    - *Behavior* - Eats junk, binge-watches TV, indulges in unhealthy habits.
    - *Impact* - Becomes dependent on fleeting pleasures, losing control over personal will.

5. The Judge
    - *Traits* - Strongly and often negatively evaluates everything, including self and others.
    - *Behavior* - Criticizes life before opening up to possibilities.
    - *Impact* - Increases isolation and struggles to trust or show care.

How to Work with These Personas

Naming and personifying your inner challenges helps you see

them as parts of yourself you can work with rather than being controlled by them.

Steps to Transform Inner Obstacles:

1. *Take Responsibility:* Recognize these behaviors and learn to address them.
2. *Understand Their Drivers:* What does each persona need?
3. *Rewrite Their Role:* Once you understand them, create a new story where you are in charge.

Thinking About Life as a Car

1. The Gas Pedal – What Drives You?

The gas pedal represents what propels us forward. However, this energy can sometimes become tension that needs to be released. Impatience creeps in as we rush to finish tasks to "move on to the next thing," or we may get caught in cycles of trying to meet our own or others' expectations. *Common "Gas Pedals" are:*

- The need to look good, impress, or please others.
- Financial expectations or unrealistic demands on oneself.
- A longing to "be someone" or to "be the man/woman."

Questions

- What is driving me forward?

- Is this energy working for me or against me?

2. The Clutch – What Gives You a Pause?

The clutch symbolizes what we do to relax or create space for ourselves. It's the part of life where we "allow" and nurture ourselves. Sometimes, however, we lose balance and turn to superficial distractions that provide little lasting value. *Common "Clutches" are:*

- Shopping to feel better (clothes, beauty products, cosmetic treatments).
- Indulging in quick fixes (junk food, sweets, alcohol).
- Numbing with screens (computers, TV, phones).

Questions

- Does my clutch truly give me rest, or is it a temporary escape?
- What could I do that nourishes me rather than numbs me?

3. The Brake – What Stops You?

The brake represents life's obstacles, whether self-imposed or external. These can include fatigue, financial strain, or physical health. Often, these obstacles stem from how we've "driven our car" up to this point. *Common "Brakes" are:*

- Exhaustion, body aches, financial difficulties.
- Cutting ties or withdrawing from challenges.
- "Switching off" through unhealthy habits (alcohol, excessive screen time).

Questions

- What in my behavior or life is stopping me now?

- Is the brake a warning that I need to reassess my speed or direction?

4. The Rearview Mirror – What Holds You Back?

The rearview mirror symbolizes the past and the baggage we carry—shame, regret, self-pity, or resentment.

While it's important to glance back and learn, staring at it too long can cause us to miss the road ahead.

Common "Rearview Mirrors" are:

- Shame over past mistakes.
- Regret over missed opportunities.
- Jealousy of others who seem better off.

Questions

- How can I learn from the past without letting it control my future?
- What do I need to let go of to focus on the road ahead?

5. The Windshield – What Do You See Ahead?

The windshield represents the future and how we envision it.

It can be clouded by fear, insecurity, or hopelessness, or it can display a clear view of possibilities and dreams, depending on how we approach today. *Common "Windshield Obstacles" are:*

- "I can't" or "It's not the right time."
- Waiting for perfect conditions to start.
- Believing you're "not enough."

Questions

- How can you clear your windshield to see the opportunities ahead?

- What can you do today to start driving toward your goals?

6. The Exhaust – What Makes Your Life Smoke?

The exhaust represents the discomfort that arises when we're out of balance. It's what happens when we've driven our car without maintenance or on the wrong path. *Common "Exhausts" are:*

- Obsessions, withdrawal symptoms, unrest.
- Powerlessness or dissatisfaction with life.

Questions

- What patterns in my life create this "exhaust"?
- How can I work on maintaining my car to reduce this strain?

7. The Tires – What Keeps You on the Road?

The tires represent what supports your journey. They are your connection to the ground and the road ahead.

If the tires are in poor condition, the journey will be short or unsafe.

Common "Tire Problems" are:

- Recklessness, imbalance, or constant breakdowns.
- Driving forward without fixing what's broken.

Questions

- How can you ensure your tires are in good condition?
- What do you need to do to create balance and make your journey safer and longer?

Final Words – The Car of Life

Life is a journey that requires maintenance, awareness, and direction. The gas pedal, clutch, brake, rearview mirror, windshield, exhaust, and tires all work together to keep you on the road.

When you learn to care for these elements, the journey becomes easier and more enjoyable.

Where do you want to go? Is your system supporting you or holding you back?

My last Story in this book - The 12-Step Program. In 2001, at the age of 27, I worked through the 12 steps of the AA program for the first time. It was a transformative experience that connected me to my spiritual core and opened doors to a better life.

I began by writing three lists:

- *Resentment List:* I noted everyone I held a grudge against—family members, an ex-girlfriend, a teacher, my boss, and a friend who had betrayed me.
- *Fear List:* I wrote down all my fears—being out of shape, always being alone, never owning anything, the police, and the tax authorities.
- *Harm List:* I listed everyone I had harmed, whether through violence or theft.

When I met with my sponsor, I shared these lists with him. Admitting the things I was ashamed of and had never dared to reveal was both difficult and uncomfortable. Yet, he shared his own experiences, helping me understand that everyone carries their own burdens.

As I walked out of the restaurant after that conversation, I felt the most incredible sensation I had ever experienced. It was as if I were directly connected to the heavens.

I felt like a spiritual being, and all my resentment and fear evaporated like dew in the morning sun.

Following this, I created my Step 9 list to make amends for my wrongs:

1. To My Ex-Girlfriend

I had treated her poorly. I reached out and told her I needed to speak with her. She immediately responded, "We're good."

However, I pointed out one particular phonecall where I had deeply wronged her. She admitted, "I always remember that when I see you."

After our conversation, that painful memory left her mind, and I felt relief for both of us.

2. To My Workplace

I had worked at a place where I stole and resold several items. After meditating on it, I found the strength to face this.

I cycled toward the company, my mind battling me every step of the way: "Don't do this!" My ego and pride didn't want to yield, but I managed to overcome them.

When I arrived, I met a kind woman who asked if I was "cleaning my garden." I confessed my wrongs and explained that I could only repay the amount in installments. She handed me an invoice for 103,975 ISK.

I went straight to the bank and paid with the last of my money. The relief was indescribable—it felt like a weight had been lifted from my shoulders.

Shortly afterward, I sold my car to the man who had purchased the stolen goods from me. He ended up stealing the car from me. Karma can be a tough teacher. 😕

. . .

The Lessons Learned

This was one of the major steps that taught me the value of truth and responsibility. Owning up to my mistakes gave me a freedom I had never experienced before. The process, though challenging, marked the beginning of a better life.

The 12-step program is a tool that most people can relate to. There are specific groups, like CoDA for co-dependency and OA for food addiction. Many churches also run 12-step programs.

For me, the journey through these steps was transformative. It was about more than recovery; it was about reclaiming my life and finding peace within myself.

Great Habits

1. *Gratitude Exercises* - Write down three things you're grateful for each day. This strengthens the mental muscle of gratitude and enhances positive emotions.

2. *Goals and Vision* - Set realistic goals and keep them in focus. This provides direction and purpose.

3. *Meditation* - Offers calm, focus, and a connection to your inner self.

4. *Aligning with Values* - Decisions rooted in your core values create a life aligned with what matters most to you.

Ways to Overcome Barriers and Establish New Habits

- *Minimize Distractions* - Take control of phone, TV, or internet use. Remove stimuli that reduce focus.
- *Preparation* - Organize workout gear, meals, or a journal the night before. This lowers resistance to starting new habits.

- *Small Steps* - Start small and build over time. A five-minute meditation or walk is a great beginning.
- *Weekly Reflection* - Schedule time weekly to review progress, adjust goals, and celebrate improvements.

Habits That Disrupt Balance

Many fall into patterns of tension that hinder physical and mental well-being. These can include:

- *Excessive caffeine or nicotine consumption* - These suppress emotions.

- *Overtraining or imbalance in exercise* - Leads to injuries or fatigue.

- *Emotional imbalance* - When tension becomes a driving force instead of well-being.

- *Unhealthy behaviors* - Overextending in relationships or giving too much of yourself without recharging.

Self-Reflecting Questions

1. What's one tool from the toolbox you can start using today?
2. What's preventing you from adopting new habits, and how can you remove those obstacles?
3. What's one small change you could make today to bring more balance and well-being into your life?

Closing Words

Healthy habits are a gift to your future self.

By consciously working on small, positive changes, you can transform your life in just a few months.

Choose one tool today and begin implementing it with intention.

Small steps lead to significant transformations!

Answer the questions and meditate for 10 minutes. Reflect on what you are sensing after this work and write it down

Notes and References

1. Time as a Precious Resource: *"Time is like a river. You cannot touch the same water twice because the flow that has passed will never pass again. Make it count!"* Attribution: This sentiment is often paraphrased but is commonly associated with the Greek philosopher Heraclitus, known for his reflections on time and change.

2. The Impact of Time Perception: Research on how time management impacts well-being. Source: Aeon, B., & Aguinis, H. (2017). *It's About Time: New Perspectives and Insights on Time Management.* Academy of Management Perspectives, 31(4), 309-330. Key insights: Time management contributes to reduced stress and increased productivity, improving overall life satisfaction.

3. Mindfulness and Time: Benefits of mindfulness in managing time and reducing stress. Source: Kabat-Zinn, J. (2003). *Mindfulness-Based Stress Reduction (MBSR).* Clinical Psychology: Science and Practice,

10(2), 144–156. Relevance: Slowing down and focusing on the present moment enhances clarity and purpose.

4. Digital Distractions and Productivity: The impact of screen time on mental clarity. Source: Mark, G., & Gonzalez, V. M. (2007). *No Task Left Behind? Examining the Nature of Fragmented Work*. Proceedings of the SIGCHI Conference on Human Factors in Computing Systems. Key finding: Excessive screen time fragments focus and leads to decreased productivity.

5. Reflection and Intentionality in Life: Philosophical reflections on time and existence. Source: Heidegger, M. (1962). *Being and Time*. (Translated by John Macquarrie & Edward Robinson). Core concept: "Time" is intrinsically tied to how individuals perceive their being and purpose.

6. The Psychology of Feeling 'Not Enough': Overcoming self-doubt to live in the present. Source: Brown, B. (2010). *The Gifts of Imperfection: Let Go of Who You Think You're Supposed to Be and Embrace Who You Are*. Hazelden Publishing. Takeaway: Embracing imperfection and self-worth is critical for overcoming the "not enough" mindset.

7. Practical Applications of Time Management: Real-life examples of intentional living. Source: Covey, S. R. (1989). *The 7 Habits of Highly Effective People: Powerful Lessons in Personal Change*. Free Press. Habit 3: "Put First Things First" emphasizes prioritizing important, non-urgent tasks.

8. The Psychological Benefits of Tracking Time: Tracking time for better life balance. Source: Vanderkam, L. (2019). *Off the Clock: Feel Less Busy While Getting More Done*. Portfolio/Penguin. Practical advice: Time-tracking can reveal patterns and opportunities for greater presence and fulfillment.

9. Living in the Present: The transformative power of living in the now. Source: Tolle, E. (1997). *The Power of Now: A Guide to Spiritual Enlightenment*. Namaste Publishing. Core idea: The present moment is the only time we truly have, and it is where life happens.

10. The Philosophy of "Perfect Moments": Maximizing the present moment. Source: Csikszentmihalyi, M. (1990). *Flow: The Psychology of Optimal Experience*. Harper & Row. Finding flow states creates profound satisfaction and connection to time and purpose.

Contagious energy and emotional influence

1. Emotional Contagion: Hatfield, E., Cacioppo, J. T., & Rapson, R. L. (1994). *Emotional Contagion*. Cambridge University Press. This work delves into how emotions spread between individuals, providing a foundation for understanding energy dynamics in social interactions.

2. Yawning and Its Contagion: Provine, R. R. (2005). *Yawning: The Anatomy of a Behavior*. American Scientist.

Attention, energy and problem-solving

1. Henry Ford's Perspective on Energy Use: While specific references to Ford's quote are scarce, works on productivity and problem-solving, such as David Allen's *Getting Things Done* (2001), align with the sentiment of focusing energy on solutions over avoidance.

2. Cognitive Load and Mental Energy: Sweller, J. (1988). *Cognitive Load During Problem Solving: Effects on Learning*. Cognitive Science. Discusses how overthinking drains mental resources, linking to the section about "mental fatigue" in the chapter.

Breaking the cycle

1. The Science of Small Actions: Fogg, B. J. (2019). *Tiny Habits: The Small Changes That Change Everything*. Houghton Mifflin Harcourt. Explains how small, intentional actions can disrupt overwhelming patterns and lead to larger changes.

2. Action Over Procrastination: Pychyl, T. A. (2013). *Solving the Procrastination Puzzle: A Concise Guide to Strategies for Change*. TarcherPerigee. Discusses how action alleviates mental burden and combats procrastination.

The Energy Pyramid

1. Holistic Energy Frameworks: Loehr, J., & Schwartz, T. (2003). *The Power of Full Engagement: Managing Energy, Not Time, Is the Key to High Performance and*

Personal Renewal. Free Press. Introduces the concept of managing energy across physical, emotional, mental, and spiritual domains.

Relaxation vs. Shutdown

1. Digital Fatigue and Mindful Consumption: Newport, C. (2019). *Digital Minimalism: Choosing a Focused Life in a Noisy World*. Portfolio. Examines how digital distractions deplete energy and suggests strategies for mindful engagement.

2. Active Relaxation Techniques: Kabat-Zinn, J. (1990). *Full Catastrophe Living: Using the Wisdom of Your Body and Mind to Face Stress, Pain, and Illness*. Delacorte Press. Provides mindfulness practices that support relaxation without leading to shutdown.

Life in Motion

1. Nature and Movement: Louv, R. (2008). *Last Child in the Woods: Saving Our Children from Nature-Deficit Disorder*. Algonquin Books. Highlights the restorative effects of nature on physical and mental energy.

2. Exercise and Mental Clarity: Ratey, J. J., & Hagerman, E. (2008). *Spark: The Revolutionary New Science of Exercise and the Brain*. Little, Brown and Company. Discusses the profound connection between movement and mental energy.

Practical Energy Management Tips

1. Tracking Energy Drains and Boosters: Rubin, G. (2015). *Better Than Before: What I Learned About Making and Breaking Habits—to Sleep More, Quit Sugar, Procrastinate Less, and Generally Build a Happier Life.* Crown. Offers methods for identifying and optimizing energy-draining versus energy-boosting habits.
2. Nutrition and Cognitive Performance: Gomez-Pinilla, F. (2008). *Brain Foods: The Effects of Nutrients on Brain Function.* Nature Reviews Neuroscience. Examines the role of diet in supporting brain energy and focus.

Flow

1. Where Attention Goes, Energy Flows: Csikszentmihalyi, M. (1990). *Flow: The Psychology of Optimal Experience.* Harper & Row. Explores the relationship between focused attention and the state of "flow" as a source of energy and productivity. The intricate connection between physical health and mental well-being is well-documented. Engaging in regular physical activity offers numerous benefits that enhance both body and mind.

Benefits of Regular Exercise

Mental Health Enhancement: Regular exercise can alleviate symptoms of depression and anxiety by regulating stress hormones and releasing mood-boosting neurotransmitters. It also promotes neuroplasticity, increasing oxygen supply to the brain, which boosts self-confidence, mood, sleep, and memory.

. . .

Healthline

- Cognitive Function Improvement: Physical activity has been shown to improve working memory, attention span, and reduce cognitive decline in adults over age 50.
- Sleep Quality Enhancement: Regular exercise can improve sleep patterns, which in turn enhances metabolic efficiency and mental focus.

HelpGuide

- Impact of Sleep on Cognitive Function:
- Memory and Attention: Adequate sleep is crucial for memory consolidation and maintaining attention. Sleep disturbances can impair these cognitive functions.
- Prioritize Quality Sleep: Aim for 7-9 hours of uninterrupted sleep to support cognitive health.

JNS Journal

- Executive Function: Sleep deprivation negatively affects decision-making and problem-solving abilities, functions primarily associated with the frontal lobe.

Oxford Academic

- Practical Recommendations: Incorporate Daily Movement: Engage in simple exercises like walking or stretching to boost mood and cognitive function.

———

Open Access Journals

- Maintain Balanced Nutrition: Consume a diet rich in whole foods to support both physical and mental health.

Medical News Today

- By integrating regular physical activity, ensuring sufficient sleep, and maintaining a balanced diet, individuals can significantly enhance their overall well-being, leading to a more fulfilling and balanced life.

Recent Insights on Physical Activity and Cognitive Health

Sources for Core Values and Personal Growth

1. Defining Core Values *Source:* Schwartz, S. H. (2012). "An Overview of the Schwartz Theory of Basic Values." *Online Readings in Psychology and Culture, 2*(1). *Summary:* Schwartz's research presents a universal model of human values, describing their role in guiding actions and shaping individual and societal behavior.

2. Self-Creation and Identity *Source:* Baumeister, R. F. (1991). *The Meanings of Life.* New York: Guilford Press. *Summary:* Baumeister explores how individuals construct meaning and identity through values and decisions, aligning with the idea that the self is created, not found.

———

The Role of Honesty in Relationships

1. Psychological and Social Benefits of Honesty *Source:* Kelly, J. M., & Yip, J. A. (2018). "Does honesty always lead to greater happiness?" *Journal of Experimental Social Psychology, 78*, 211-222. *Summary:* This study explores the impact of honesty on emotional well-being, emphasizing the relational benefits of transparency and trust.

2. Truth and Liberation *Source:* Campbell, J. (1988). *The Power of Myth.* New York: Doubleday. *Summary:* Joseph Campbell discusses how living authentically and truthfully can lead to personal liberation and spiritual growth.

Family and Values

1. The Role of Family in Core Values Formation *Source:* Bengtson, V. L., & Roberts, R. E. L. (1991). "Intergenerational Solidarity in Aging Families: An Example of Formal Theory Construction." *Journal of Marriage and Family, 53*(4), 856–870. *Summary:* This article examines the transmission of core values within families and their influence on intergenerational relationships.

2. Love and Emotional Reciprocity in Family Dynamics *Source:* Gottman, J. M., & Silver, N. (1999). *The Seven Principles for Making Marriage Work.* New York: Harmony Books. *Summary:* Gottman emphasizes the importance of reciprocal emotional investment and respect in strengthening family ties.

Respect and Boundary Setting

1. Respect in Interpersonal Relationships *Source:* Hall, J. A., & Fincham, F. D. (2005). "Self-Respect and Other-Respect: The Moral, Emotional, and Spiritual Dimensions of Respect." *The Journal of Positive Psychology, 2*(2), 97-117. *Summary:* This paper highlights the necessity of self-respect and respect for others in fostering healthy relationships and personal well-being.

2. Boundaries and Mental Health *Source:* Cloud, H., & Townsend, J. (1992). *Boundaries: When to Say Yes, How to Say No to Take Control of Your Life.* Grand Rapids: Zondervan. *Summary:* This book explores how setting and maintaining boundaries is key to emotional and mental health.

Practical Insights and Applications

1. Meditation and Values *Source:* Kabat-Zinn, J. (1994). *Wherever You Go, There You Are: Mindfulness Meditation in Everyday Life.* Hyperion. *Summary:* Kabat-Zinn's work on mindfulness and meditation can provide tools for aligning daily actions with core values.

2. Behavioral Alignment with Values *Source:* Hayes, S. C., Strosahl, K. D., & Wilson, K. G. (1999). *Acceptance and Commitment Therapy: An Experiential Approach to Behavior Change.* Guilford Press. *Summary:* This book offers practical exercises for aligning behaviors with values to create meaningful changes in life.

The Journey of Growth and Inner Change

1. Life as a Journey *Source:* Frankl, V. E. (2006). *Man's Search for Meaning.* Beacon Press. *Summary:* Viktor Frankl explores how finding purpose in life and enduring suffering leads to personal growth and fulfillment.

2. The Courage to Change *Source:* Brown, B. (2012). *Daring Greatly: How the Courage to Be Vulnerable Transforms the Way We Live, Love, Parent, and Lead.* Gotham Books. *Summary:* Brown delves into how vulnerability is a pathway to courage, creativity, and change.

3. Breaking Patterns *Source:* Prochaska, J. O., Norcross, J. C., & DiClemente, C. C. (1994). *Changing for Good: A Revolutionary Six-Stage Program for Overcoming Bad Habits and Moving Your Life Positively Forward.* HarperCollins. *Summary:* This book introduces the stages of change model, offering strategies for breaking free from harmful patterns and fostering growth.

Understanding Resistance to Change

1. The Psychology of Resistance *Source:* Jung, C. G. (1961). *Memories, Dreams, Reflections.* Vintage Books. *Summary:* Jung reflects on the unconscious mind's role in shaping human behavior and how resistance arises from fear of confronting our deeper selves.

2. The Neuroscience of Change *Source:* Kahneman, D. (2011). *Thinking, Fast and Slow.* Farrar, Straus, and

Giroux. *Summary:* Kahneman discusses how our brain's systems for decision-making influence resistance to change and growth.

Letting Go and Embracing New Opportunities

1. The Art of Letting Go *Source:* Tolle, E. (2004). *The Power of Now: A Guide to Spiritual Enlightenment.* New World Library. *Summary:* Tolle explains how living in the present moment frees individuals from the burdens of the past and fears of the future.
2. Courage to Take Risks*Source:* Ryan, R. M., & Deci, E. L. (2000). "Self-determination theory and the facilitation of intrinsic motivation, social development, and well-being." *American Psychologist, 55*(1), 68–78.
3. *Summary:* This article explores the role of intrinsic motivation and autonomy in taking risks and embracing personal growth.

Repetition and Behavior Shaping

1. The Role of Habits in Change *Source:* Clear, J. (2018). *Atomic Habits: An Easy & Proven Way to Build Good Habits & Break Bad Ones.* Avery. *Summary:* Clear emphasizes the importance of small, consistent changes and how repetition forms lasting habits.

2. Behavior and Meaning *Source:* Csikszentmihalyi, M. (1990). *Flow: The Psychology of Optimal Experience.* Harper & Row. *Summary:* This work discusses how engaging in meaningful activities through deliberate effort leads to fulfillment and growth.

Inspirational and Philosophical Perspectives

1. Life as a Reality to Be Experienced. *Source:* Kierkegaard, S. (1980). *The Sickness Unto Death: A Christian Psychological Exposition for Upbuilding and Awakening.* Princeton University Press. *Summary:* Kierkegaard explores existential themes of despair, self-discovery, and embracing life's experiences.

2. Facing Challenges and Building Resilience *Source:* Duckworth, A. (2016). *Grit: The Power of Passion and Perseverance.* Scribner. *Summary:* Duckworth highlights how perseverance and passion drive success and help overcome resistance to growth.

Practical Applications

1. Self-Reflection Practices *Source:* Kabat-Zinn, J. (1990). *Full Catastrophe Living: Using the Wisdom of Your Body and Mind to Face Stress, Pain, and Illness.* Bantam Dell. *Summary:* This book provides mindfulness techniques to overcome resistance and focus on intentional living.

2. Overcoming Fear of Change *Source:* Robbins, A. (2001). *Awaken the Giant Within: How to Take Immediate Control of Your Mental, Emotional, Physical, and Financial Destiny!* Free Press. *Summary:* Robbins outlines actionable strategies to address fear and embrace opportunities for personal transformation.

Inspirational Quotes

- Voltaire's Perspective on Aimless Action: Voltaire, F. M. A. (1764). "Dictionnaire philosophique."
- *Summary:* Voltaire critiques purposeless ambition and emphasizes the need for clarity in direction and purpose.
- Carl Jung on Avoiding the Soul: *Source:* Jung, C. G. (1957). *The Undiscovered Self.* Princeton University Press. *Summary:* Jung explores how societal and individual avoidance of inner truths stifles personal growth.

Foundational Concepts in Communication

1. The Importance of Listening *Source:* Covey, S. R. (1989). *The 7 Habits of Highly Effective People.* Free Press. *Summary:* Covey emphasizes the principle, "Seek first to understand, then to be understood," as a cornerstone of effective communication and trust-building.

2. Self-Centeredness and Connection *Source:* Goleman, D. (2006). *Social Intelligence: The New Science of Human Relationships.* Bantam Books. *Summary:* Goleman explores how emotional and social intelligence influence connection and how self-centered behaviors can erode relationships.

3. The Role of Perspective in Understanding *Source:* Rogers, C. R. (1961). *On Becoming a Person: A Therapist's View of Psychotherapy.* Houghton Mifflin. *Summary:* Rogers discusses empathy and the importance of seeing the world through others' perspectives for genuine connection.

Self-Awareness and Emotional Responsibility

1. Emotional Self-Regulation *Source:* Gross, J. J. (2014). "Emotion regulation: Conceptual and empirical foundations." *Handbook of Emotion Regulation.* *Summary:* This research highlights how managing emotional responses improves communication and relationships.
2. Accountability for Emotional Reactions *Source:* Brown, B. (2010). *The Gifts of Imperfection: Let Go of Who You Think You're Supposed to Be and Embrace Who You Are.* Hazelden. *Summary:* Brown explores the importance of emotional accountability in fostering healthy self-expression and relationships.

Building Trust and Effective Communication

1. Integrity and Truth in Relationships *Source:* Tolle, E. (2004). *The Power of Now: A Guide to Spiritual Enlightenment.* New World Library. *Summary:* Tolle discusses the role of truth and presence in fostering trust and meaningful connections.

2. Nurturing Healthy Communication *Source:* Chapman, G. (1992). *The Five Love Languages: How to Express Heartfelt Commitment to Your Mate.* Northfield Publishing. *Summary:* Chapman introduces the idea of personalized communication styles that strengthen relationships by addressing emotional needs.

3. Understanding Perspectives *Source:* Stone, D., Patton, B., & Heen, S. (1999). *Difficult Conversations: How to Discuss What Matters Most.* Penguin Books. *Summary:* This book provides insights on navigating

challenging conversations and understanding others' perspectives.

Impact of Words and Toxic Patterns

1. The Power of Words *Source:* Peterson, J. B. (2018). *12 Rules for Life: An Antidote to Chaos.* Random House Canada. *Summary:* Peterson emphasizes using clear, honest communication to build integrity and order in relationships.

2. Breaking Toxic Communication Cycles. *Source:* Gottman, J., & Silver, N. (1999). *The Seven Principles for Making Marriage Work.* Harmony Books. *Summary:* Gottman outlines how addressing toxic patterns in communication can repair and strengthen relationships.

Practical Tools for Communication

1. Steps to Improve Communication *Source:* Rosenberg, M. B. (2003). *Nonviolent Communication: A Language of Life.* PuddleDancer Press. *Summary:* Rosenberg provides strategies for improving communication by focusing on empathy, honesty, and mutual understanding.

2. Maintaining Balance in Communication *Source:* Siegel, D. J. (2010). *Mindsight: The New Science of Personal Transformation.* Bantam Books. *Summary:* Siegel discusses the role of mindfulness in enhancing emotional balance and communication effectiveness.

Inspirational Perspectives

1. Oscar Wilde's Quote on Changing Others *Source:* Wilde, O. (1891). *The Soul of Man under Socialism.*
2. *Summary:* Wilde critiques societal tendencies to focus on altering others rather than improving oneself. Connection vs. Correction *Source:* Satir, V. (1972). *Peoplemaking.* Science and Behavior Books. *Summary:* Satir highlights how fostering connection, rather than enforcing correction, deepens trust and relationships.

Reflections on Respect and Boundaries

1. Respect in Communication *Source:* Arbinger Institute. (2002). *Leadership and Self-Deception: Getting Out of the Box.* Berrett-Koehler Publishers. *Summary:* The book explores how self-deception undermines respect and the importance of seeing others as equals in communication.

2. Setting Healthy Boundaries *Source:* Cloud, H., & Townsend, J. (1992). *Boundaries: When to Say Yes, How to Say No to Take Control of Your Life.* Zondervan. *Summary:* Cloud and Townsend offer tools for creating and maintaining boundaries to enhance respect and self-worth.

Foundational Concepts in Healthy Communication

1. Mindful Listening *Source:* Covey, S. R. (1989). *The 7 Habits of Highly Effective People.* Free Press. *Summary:* Covey's principle "Seek first to understand, then to be understood" emphasizes the power of

mindful listening and creating an open space for connection.

2. The Role of Warmth and Belonging in Relationships *Source:* Maslow, A. H. (1943). "A Theory of Human Motivation." *Psychological Review*. *Summary:* Maslow's hierarchy of needs highlights belonging and love as essential for psychological well-being and healthy communication.

3. Boundaries and Emotional Safety *Source:* Cloud, H., & Townsend, J. (1992). *Boundaries: When to Say Yes, How to Say No to Take Control of Your Life.* Zondervan. *Summary:* The authors discuss setting respectful boundaries to protect emotional balance and strengthen self-respect.

Understanding the Impact of Control in Relationships

1. The Dynamics of Control and Communication *Source:* Goleman, D. (1995). *Emotional Intelligence: Why It Can Matter More Than IQ.* Bantam Books. *Summary:* Goleman explores how emotions influence behavior, including control dynamics and their effect on interpersonal communication.

2. Walking Away from Harmful Relationships *Source:* Brown, B. (2012). *Daring Greatly: How the Courage to be Vulnerable Transforms the Way We Live, Love, Parent, and Lead.* Avery. *Summary:* Brown emphasizes the importance of vulnerability in relationships and the courage to set boundaries when relationships threaten self-worth.

―――――

Building Connections Through Respect and Awareness

1. Healthy Communication Practices *Source:* Rosenberg, M. B. (2003). *Nonviolent Communication: A Language of Life.* PuddleDancer Press. *Summary:* Rosenberg introduces strategies for empathetic and respectful communication to build understanding and reduce conflict.

2. Empathy and Emotional Awareness *Source:* Siegel, D. J. (2010). *Mindsight: The New Science of Personal Transformation.* Bantam Books. *Summary:* Siegel discusses the importance of emotional awareness in fostering meaningful and empathetic connections.

Stories and Examples from Daily Life

1. The Power of Letting Go in Relationships *Source:* Tolle, E. (2004). *The Power of Now: A Guide to Spiritual Enlightenment.* New World Library. *Summary:* Tolle explores how releasing past attachments and practicing presence can transform relationships and reduce stress.

2. Family Dynamics and Communication Challenges *Source:* Bowen, M. (1978). *Family Therapy in Clinical Practice.* Jason Aronson. *Summary:* Bowen's family systems theory highlights the complexities of family relationships and how unresolved emotional dynamics influence communication.

Practical Techniques for Improving Communication

1. Confidence in Communication *Source:* Patterson, K., Grenny, J., McMillan, R., & Switzler, A. (2002).

Crucial Conversations: Tools for Talking When Stakes Are High. McGraw-Hill. *Summary:* This book provides actionable tools for navigating difficult conversations with clarity and confidence.

2. The Importance of Respectful Boundaries *Source:* Arbinger Institute. (2002). *Leadership and Self-Deception: Getting Out of the Box.* Berrett-Koehler Publishers. *Summary:* The authors explore how respect and self-awareness improve interpersonal dynamics and communication.

Inspirational and Theoretical Foundations

1. Sowell's Perspective on Honesty in Communication *Source:* Sowell, T. (2007). *A Conflict of Visions: Ideological Origins of Political Struggles.* Basic Books. *Summary:* Sowell discusses how ideological perspectives shape communication and decision-making.

2. Emotional Triggers in Communication *Source:* Jung, C. G. (1964). *Man and His Symbols.* Doubleday. *Summary:* Jung explores how unconscious emotions and archetypes influence communication and interpersonal behavior.

Practical Steps for Growth

1. Self-Reflection in Communication *Source:* Satir, V. (1972). *Peoplemaking.* Science and Behavior Books. *Summary:* Satir highlights the role of self-reflection in improving communication and building healthier relationships.

2. Aligning Words with Actions *Source:* Peterson, J. B. (2018). *12 Rules for Life: An Antidote to Chaos.* Random House Canada. *Summary:* Peterson emphasizes taking responsibility for one's words and actions to create meaningful connections.

Psychological Foundations of the Inner Judge

1. The Inner Critic and Self-Compassion *Source:* Neff, K. D. (2011). *Self-Compassion: Stop Beating Yourself Up and Leave Insecurity Behind.* HarperCollins. *Summary:* Neff explains the origins of the inner critic and offers tools to cultivate self-compassion, which alleviates the harsh judgment we often direct toward ourselves.

2. The Role of Childhood Experiences in Shaping Judgment *Source:* Siegel, D. J. (2012). *The Developing Mind: How Relationships and the Brain Interact to Shape Who We Are.* Guilford Press. *Summary:* Siegel discusses how early environments and attachment styles influence the development of self-critical voices and judgmental patterns.

3. Understanding the "Judge" in Context of Personality Structures *Source:* Berne, E. (1964). *Games People Play: The Psychology of Human Relationships.* Grove Press. *Summary:* Berne's Parent-Adult-Child model offers insight into how the "Parent" (often critical) voice develops and operates in our interactions with ourselves and others.

Tools for Addressing and Transforming the Inner Judge

1. Mindfulness and the Observing Self *Source:* Kabat-Zinn, J. (1990). *Full Catastrophe Living: Using the Wisdom of Your Body and Mind to Face Stress, Pain, and Illness.* Bantam Books. *Summary:* Kabat-Zinn provides mindfulness techniques to step back from judgmental thoughts and cultivate non-reactive awareness.

2. Cognitive Behavioral Approaches to Challenge the Judge *Source:* Burns, D. D. (1989). *The Feeling Good Handbook.* Plume. *Summary:* Burns introduces strategies to identify and reframe negative thought patterns, including self-critical judgments.

Philosophical and Ethical Insights

1. The Dangers of Judgment in Human Interaction *Source:* Kierkegaard, S. (1849). *The Sickness Unto Death.* Princeton University Press. *Summary:* Kierkegaard explores how judgment can separate individuals from their authentic selves, creating despair and alienation.

2. The Power of Forgiveness *Source:* Enright, R. D., & Fitzgibbons, R. P. (2000). *Helping Clients Forgive: An Empirical Guide for Resolving Anger and Restoring Hope.* American Psychological Association. *Summary:* The authors discuss forgiveness as a transformative process for releasing judgment and fostering emotional freedom.

The Role of Compassion and Understanding

1. Compassion for Others as a Path to Healing *Source:* Nhat Hanh, T. (2004). *No Mud, No Lotus: The Art of Transforming Suffering.* Parallax Press. *Summary:* Thich Nhat Hanh emphasizes the importance of understanding and compassion for both self and others in overcoming suffering and judgment.

2. Forgiveness as Liberation *Source:* Luskin, F. (2002). *Forgive for Good: A Proven Prescription for Health and Happiness.* HarperOne. *Summary:* Luskin outlines steps to forgiveness, explaining how letting go of judgment creates inner peace and healthier relationships.

Practical Techniques for Overcoming Judgment

1. The Practice of Nonviolent Communication *Source:* Rosenberg, M. B. (2003). *Nonviolent Communication: A Language of Life.* PuddleDancer Press. *Summary:* Rosenberg offers methods for communicating with empathy and understanding, reducing judgment and conflict in interactions.

2. Transforming Perception Through Gratitude *Source:* Emmons, R. A. (2007). *Thanks! How the New Science of Gratitude Can Make You Happier.* Houghton Mifflin. *Summary:* Emmons discusses how cultivating gratitude shifts focus away from judgment and toward appreciation and connection.

———

Inspirational Perspectives and Quotes

1. "Judge Not, That Ye Be Not Judged" *Source:* Holy Bible, *Matthew 7:1-2*. *Summary:* A timeless reminder of how judgment reflects back on the judge, encouraging humility and introspection.

2. Understanding vs. Judging *Source:* Jung, C. G. (1933). *Modern Man in Search of a Soul*. Harcourt. *Summary:* Jung emphasizes the importance of understanding the unconscious mind rather than judging its complexities.

Stories and Reflection Tools

1. Shame and Vulnerability *Source:* Brown, B. (2010). *The Gifts of Imperfection: Let Go of Who You Think You're Supposed to Be and Embrace Who You Are*. Hazelden. *Summary:* Brown explores how shame and judgment inhibit growth, and how embracing vulnerability fosters connection and authenticity.

2. Reframing Failure and Judgment *Source:* Dweck, C. S. (2006). *Mindset: The New Psychology of Success*. Ballantine Books. *Summary:* Dweck introduces the concept of a growth mindset, showing how reframing failure and judgment leads to personal and professional success.

The Psychology of Numbing and Addiction

1. Addiction as Emotional Avoidance*Source:* Maté, G. (2010). *In the Realm of Hungry Ghosts: Close Encounters with Addiction*. North Atlantic Books.*Summary:*

Gabor Maté explores the roots of addiction, emphasizing that addictive behaviors often stem from pain and serve as a means to numb emotional wounds.

2. The Science of Numbing and Emotional Pain *Source:* Levine, P. A. (2010). *In an Unspoken Voice: How the Body Releases Trauma and Restores Goodness.* North Atlantic Books. *Summary:* Levine discusses how numbing manifests as a survival mechanism, disconnecting individuals from both their pain and their true selves.

3. The Role of Avoidance in Addiction *Source:* Hayes, S. C., Strosahl, K. D., & Wilson, K. G. (1999). *Acceptance and Commitment Therapy: An Experiential Approach to Behavior Change.* Guilford Press. *Summary:* This text introduces Acceptance and Commitment Therapy (ACT), focusing on how avoidance sustains harmful patterns and how mindful engagement helps break the cycle.

Transformation and Hope

1. The Role of Hope in Recovery *Source:* Lynch, W. F. (1965). *Images of Hope: Imagination as Healer of the Hopeless.* University of Notre Dame Press. *Summary:* Lynch explores hope as a necessary element for overcoming despair and finding meaning in life's challenges.

2. Facing Pain and Transformation *Source:* Campbell, J. (1949). *The Hero with a Thousand Faces.* Princeton University Press. *Summary:* Campbell's concept of the hero's journey highlights the transformative

power of facing inner challenges and embracing growth.

Breaking Patterns of Addiction

1. Understanding Addiction's Cycle *Source:* Prochaska, J. O., Norcross, J. C., & DiClemente, C. C. (1994). *Changing for Good: A Revolutionary Six-Stage Program for Overcoming Bad Habits and Moving Your Life Positively Forward.* William Morrow Paperbacks. *Summary:* The authors outline the stages of change and provide actionable steps for breaking destructive habits and creating positive behaviors.

2. The Body Craves What It Contains *Source:* Marlatt, G. A., & Donovan, D. M. (Eds.). (2005). *Relapse Prevention: Maintenance Strategies in the Treatment of Addictive Behaviors.* Guilford Press. *Summary:* This book examines how habitual cravings and environmental triggers maintain addiction and offers strategies for relapse prevention.

Mindfulness and Conscious Living

1. Mindfulness as a Path to Freedom *Source:* Kabat-Zinn, J. (2005). *Coming to Our Senses: Healing Ourselves and the World Through Mindfulness.* Hyperion. *Summary:* Kabat-Zinn emphasizes mindfulness as a tool to stay present, confront discomfort, and break free from avoidance patterns.

2. The Power of Conscious Thought *Source:* Allen, J. (1911). *As a Man Thinketh.* Grosset & Dunlap.
3. *Summary:* Allen explores how conscious thought

shapes behavior, offering insights into how intentional thinking fosters positive change.

Courage and Letting Go

1. Letting Go of Old Patterns *Source:* Frankl, V. E. (1946). *Man's Search for Meaning.* Beacon Press.
2. *Summary:* Frankl discusses the importance of finding meaning and letting go of limiting beliefs and attachments to transform suffering into growth.//
3. Stepping into the Unknown *Source:* Brown, B. (2012). *Daring Greatly: How the Courage to Be Vulnerable Transforms the Way We Live, Love, Parent, and Lead.* Gotham Books. *Summary:* Brown examines how embracing vulnerability and courage leads to deeper connections and personal freedom.

Addiction, Temptation, and Control

1. The Science of Temptation and Willpower *Source:* Baumeister, R. F., & Tierney, J. (2011). *Willpower: Rediscovering the Greatest Human Strength.* Penguin Press. *Summary:* Baumeister explores the mechanisms of self-control and how building willpower helps overcome temptations and harmful habits.
2. The Role of Self-Discipline in Recovery *Source:* Ryan, R. M., & Deci, E. L. (2000). *Self-Determination Theory and the Facilitation of Intrinsic Motivation, Social Development, and Well-Being.* American

Psychologist. *Summary:* This paper discusses how fostering autonomy and intrinsic motivation strengthens resilience and supports long-term recovery.

Inspirational and Philosophical Insights

1. Living with Authenticity and Freedom *Source:* Kierkegaard, S. (1849). *The Sickness Unto Death.* Princeton University Press. *Summary:* Kierkegaard explores the concept of despair and the path to authenticity by confronting uncomfortable truths.

2. The Courage to Move Beyond Familiar Shores *Source:* Faulkner, W. (1952). *Requiem for a Nun.* Vintage Books. *Summary:* Faulkner's quote about losing sight of the shore captures the essence of courage required to embrace transformation.

Addiction as a Developmental Process

1. Source: Volkow, N. D., & Koob, G. F. (2015). "Neurocircuitry of Addiction." *Neuropsychopharmacology.* This paper explores how addiction develops as a process of changes in brain circuitry and its relationship to behavior. Link: Neuropsychopharmacology Article

2. Source: American Society of Addiction Medicine (ASAM). ASAM's definition of addiction as a treatable, chronic medical disease influenced by interactions among brain circuits, genetics, environment, and individual life experiences. Link: ASAM's Definition

Why We Numb Ourselves

3. Source: Maté, G. (2008). *In the Realm of Hungry Ghosts: Close Encounters with Addiction*. Gabor Maté explores the connection between unresolved emotional pain and addiction, emphasizing how early-life trauma influences dependency.

4. Source: Porges, S. W. (2011). *The Polyvagal Theory: Neurophysiological Foundations of Emotions, Attachment, Communication, and Self-Regulation*. Explains how emotional regulation is often disrupted in those who seek to numb themselves, tying to the neurobiology of shame and trauma.

Temptations and Self-Discipline

5. Source: Baumeister, R. F., Vohs, K. D., & Tice, D. M. (2007). "The Strength Model of Self-Control." *Current Directions in Psychological Science*. This article discusses self-control as a finite resource and the role of discipline in overcoming temptations. Link: Current Directions Article.

6. Source: Kelly, J. F., & White, W. L. (2011). *Addiction Recovery Management: Theory, Research, and Practice*. This book provides practical frameworks for addiction recovery and strategies for building resilience.

The Path to Self-Integrity and Healing

1. Source: Brown, B. (2012). *Daring Greatly: How the Courage to Be Vulnerable Transforms the Way We Live, Love, Parent, and Lead*. Discusses how

vulnerability and authenticity are key to healing and overcoming shame, often core drivers of addiction.

2. Source: Miller, W. R., & Rollnick, S. (2012). *Motivational Interviewing: Helping People Change.*

Provides strategies for helping individuals explore their internal motivations for change, essential in addressing addiction.

Poetry and Philosophy as Insightful Tools

1. Source: Rumi. Translations by Coleman Barks in *The Essential Rumi* (1995). Rumi's insights on searching inward for growth and transformation provide spiritual parallels to addiction recovery.

2. Source: Jonsson, J. E. (2001). "Poetry as Therapy: Insights from Icelandic Literature." *Nordic Journal of Psychiatry*. Explores how poetic metaphors resonate with mental health and healing journeys.

Suggested Additions for Research

- Explore *Self-Determination Theory (SDT)* by Deci and Ryan for insights into how intrinsic motivation impacts long-term recovery.
- Look into the 12-Step Program Literature, such as Alcoholics Anonymous (AA), which emphasizes spiritual growth and accountability in addiction recovery.